SANGRANDO POR LOS 5 SENTIDOS

BLEEDING FROM ALL 5 SENSES

Mario Santiago Papasquiaro

Translated by Cole Heinowitz

WHITE PINE PRESS / BUFFALO, NEW YORK

White Pine Press
P.O. Box 236
Buffalo, NY 14201
www.whitepine.org

These pieces were published in the Spanish in:
  "Manifiesto infrarrealista." *Perros habitados por las voces del desierto*. Ed. Rubén Medina. Matadero, 2014.
  Respiración del laberinto. La Ratona Cartonera, 2010.
  Jeta de santo (Antología Poética, 1974-1997). Fondo de Cultura Económica de España, 2008.
  Aullido de cisne. Al Este del Paraíso, 1996.
  "Seis jóvenes infrarrealistas mexicanos." *Plural* n. 63 (December, 1976).

The translations originally appered in:
"Infra Correspondence" and "Saint Malcolm X" - *The Common*. "Single Blood" - *Harper's Magazine*. "Bizarre Clarity," "Relentless Song," "Mariana Larrosa Appears," and "The Sons of King Lopitos" - *A Perfect Vacuum*. "Open Letter to Kenneth Rexroth," "Did You Notice How the Seine Doesn't Look Us in the Eye Anymore," "To Our Lady of Guadalumpen," and "Carte d'Identité" - *Exchanges: Journal of Literary Translation*. "Second-Hand Heroes" - *The Wave Papers*. "Imitation of Li Po," "Steal Fire from the Devil," and "Ecce Homo" - *Two Lines*. "Saint John of the Cross Does 1 Solo for Neal Cassady / on the Border between Myth & Dream /," "[The Sleepwalking Assassin]," "Dead End Street," and "Abyssinia's Shock" - *Riot of Perfume*. "I Fly Overhead Nonetheless Like 1 Dynasty of Suns," "Swan's Howl," "Dismirror," and "I Walk to Teotitlán del Camino Even on the Metro San Lázaro" - *Dolce Stil Criollo*. "Vision in Sinai" and "Leap Year Adolescence" - The Poetry Society of America, "In Their Own Words." "Already Far from the Road" - *Clock*.

Publication of this book was made possible, in part, with funds from The Amazon Literary Partnership. .

Printed and bound in the United States of America.

ISBN 978-1-945680-31-1

Library of Congress Control Number: 2018968432

Sangrando por los 5 sentidos

Bleeding from All 5 Senses

Table of Contents

INTRODUCTION

Born in the Mixcoac area of Mexico City on December 24, 1953, Mario Santiago Papasquiaro came of age during the period of ruthless political repression known as the Dirty War. The late 1960s were also a time of revolutionary ferment in Mexico, a time when hundreds of thousands of workers, artists, students, and intellectuals took to the streets to demand change. As the government made lavish preparations for the 1968 Mexico City Olympics, public dissent intensified. Tensions reached a crisis on October 2, when roughly 10,000 high-school students, university students, and other peaceful protesters who had gathered in the *Plaza de las Tres Culturas* were surrounded by military tanks, helicopters, and armed troops that opened fire on the crowd, killing hundreds.

Even in a climate in which dissent was routinely suppressed and state-sponsored killings had become almost a commonplace, the government's illegal massacre of these protesters sent shockwaves through a generation. According to Mexican law, it was not a crime to publicly express or to publish one's opinions. But if one's opinions diverged from those of the ruling party, the PRI (*Partido Revolucionario Institucional*), access to the cultural platforms and media channels for disseminating those ideas was out of the question. When he started writing seriously in the early 1970s, Santiago Papasquiaro was well aware that he would have to create a context for his work outside the tightly-policed borders of the academy and the official literary establishment.

In 1973, Santiago Papasquiaro gave his first public reading and, in early 1974, he published *Zarazo*, a tabloid-format journal combining Surrealist and Dada texts with contemporary Marxist theory and works by the Beats and the experimental Peruvian poets of *Hora Zero*. A year later, he met the young Chilean Roberto Bolaño and, along with a handful of friends and co-conspirators, founded the radical poetry movement, Infrarealism. Bound together by their resistance to the dominant artistic, literary, and political culture, the Infras spurned institutional acceptance and professional advancement, committing themselves instead to the uncompromising integration of art and life at all costs. This commitment took many forms, from endless walks through the city declaiming their poems to sabotaging the lectures, book releases, and cocktail parties of prominent literati. As a result, the Infras were condemned by Mexico's cultural élites as a group of puerile, ignorant, depraved troublemakers.

In 1977, following the advice of André Breton's "Surrealist Manifesto," Santiago Papasquiaro decided to "drop everything" and "take to the road." He was a thief in Paris, a dishwasher in Barcelona, a fruit picker in Lérida, a fisherman in Port-Vendres, a political prisoner in Vienna, and a kibbutznik in Israel. When he returned home at the end of the decade, Mexican literary society was unchanged, and as hostile to him as ever. He wandered the labyrinths of Mexico City day and night, reading voraciously, composing aloud, and writing, always writing as he walked—in the margins of borrowed books and the pages of newspapers, on flyers, magazines, receipts, coasters, napkins, matchbooks, paper bags—on any available surface, however impermanent. Poetry was not simply a vocation or a passion for Santiago Papasquiaro; it was his way of moving through life, of sensing and physically collaborating with the currents and convulsions of the world. It was, as he wrote in his 1975 "Infrarealist Manifesto," the total fusion of art and life, the realization of Antonin Artaud's demand for "a culture in the flesh."

Although publication was a largely secondary consideration for Santiago Papasquiaro, a number of important works appeared in independent magazines and anthologies throughout the 1970s and 1980s, beginning with his groundbreaking long poem of 1975, *Consejos de 1 discípulo de Marx a 1 fanático de Heidegger* [*Advice from 1 Disciple of Marx to 1 Heidegger Fanatic*]. In 1994, Santiago Papasquiaro and the journalist Marco Lara Klahr created the imprint Al Este del Paraíso [East of Eden], which subsequently released the only two books to be published during his lifetime, *Beso eterno* [*Eternal Kiss*] (1995) and *Aullido de cisne* [*Swan's Howl*] (1996). On January 10, 1998, Santiago Papasquiaro was hit by a car and killed on one of his habitual rambles through the streets of Mexico City.

In the years since his death, several volumes have appeared that begin to reveal the full extent of Santiago Papasquiaro's poetic output, most notably the collection *Jeta de santo* (2008), co-edited by Mario Raúl Guzmán and the poet's widow, Rebeca López. Critical appreciations and translations of his work have multiplied in recent years and his impact on a rising generation of poets can be seen across Mexico, as well as in Chile and the Unites States. Santiago Papasquiaro's presence also continues to inform the work of those writers who had the good fortune to know and interact with him in person—among them, Roberto Bolaño, Carmen Boullosa, Rubén Medina, Guadalupe Ochoa, José Peguero, and Juan Villoro. Without doubt, Santiago Papasquiaro's searing irreverence, full-throated lyricism, and wild lucidity are as urgently necessary today as they were in 1975. His work forcibly reminds us that even if "we forget it / overwhelmed by the pain of not knowing ourselves ... 1 poem is occurring every moment ... & with every appearance of becoming Epic History" (*Advice from 1 Disciple of Marx to 1 Heidegger Fanatic*).

A, E, I, O, U. The rhythmic concatenation of these five vowels is the tachycardic pulse of Mario Santiago Papasquiaro's poetry, and it cannot be imitated in English. Feeling for correlative patterns in the jangle of our consonant-frontal idiom is something like transcribing the pitch values of a Max Roach drum solo for honkytonk piano. I do what I can with alliteration, but even the relatively long decay of the M or the out-hissing S does not match the multi-textured overtones of a hard O spilling through the rails of its word-cage, trailing a foam of soft E's across the rubble.

When I was a girl, I had chronic pneumonia, which always came with very high fevers. Lying in bed at night, I'd be certain I heard a full orchestra playing a Beethoven symphony or a rock band playing Stones covers in the house next door. When I'd call my mother in to listen, she'd invariably say, "that's just a train going by" or "that's just the boiler rumbling in the basement." Much like the way these fevers magically revealed the harmonies implicit in what we generally think of as noise, reading and translating Mario has changed how I hear.

As a reader, I listen into his rhythms and watch the shapes they trace in my mind. As a translator, I lean into the rhythms much more blindly, and it is only when absolutely necessary that I will try to see an image clearly or consciously grasp the implications of a metaphor. This may be a useful stance in general for the translator, but I mean it in a very particular sense in the case of Santiago Papasquiaro. Like a sick person touched by a healer or a violin inevitably detuning toward the natural intervals of sound, or maybe more like a radio locking in on a signal, I feel my heartbeat synchronize to the more coherent frequency.

But Santiago Papasquiaro's poetry is neither "natural" nor "coherent" in the conventional sense of these words. When he was scouring Mexico City (or Barcelona, or Paris...) at all hours of the day, for days on end, I think he was "tuning" himself the way a string can be tuned to the dominant or most proximate frequency. But unlike a cello or a broadcast receiver, Santiago Papasquiaro was tuning to an-ever shifting, fundamentally incoherent target. What's more, he con-tained—and perpetually emitted—a powerfully erratic electro-magnetic charge as seemingly autonomous as the city's.

This vibrational face-off between a so-called "self" and a so-called "other" is challenging for me because, like Santiago Papasquiaro, I reject the distinction. Another challenge is the astonishing range and specificity of his vocabulary—spanning from Náhuatl to German phenomenology and from Cold War bureau-cant to '70s Chilango street slang. As a translator, there are many moments when all dic-tionaries seem to be colluding to expunge whole swaths of human history from the record. This is where one of the translator's great unsung virtues—fragile personal boundaries—comes into play. I feel my heart inside my chest; it is beating very fast and very hard. "Do you know what Mario is saying?" I ask my heart. Here are its an-swers.

Sangrando por los 5 sentidos

Bleeding from All 5 Senses

For Mowgli & Nadja Zendejas

HÉROES DE OCASIÓN: SEIS JÓVENES INFRARREALISTAS MEXICANOS

Por un arte quitasueño / contra un arte adormidera
César Moro

Había decidido aplastarlos y dejarlos a 1 cm. de piso...
pero me faltó la cinta métrica
Groucho Marx

A Groucho,
Chico & Harpo
para que se sientan
fuera de lugar

En 1968: menos de 15 años de edad / veían series gringas por T.V. / soldados en las calles / comunistas de carne y hueso agitando en plena vía pública. De ahí para adelante: la experiencia viva, la pesadilla viva, la utopía viva / La emoción, la sensación, la certeza de bucear por grietas a cada momento transformándose / Vagabundos radicales, prófugos de la universidad burguesa (la mediocridad de la enseñanza es la enseñanza de la mediocridad). Han recorrido autopistas, selvas, playas donde el H. Departamento de Turismo pescaría por lo menos un resfriado "underground" / & los han gaseado, macaneado, correteado, & han sostenido su puño en alto, bromeando alrededor de PERDEDORES POWER. La poesía (la retórica que se paseaba con ese nombre) no los inmiscuía para nada / Becerra, Pacheco jamás pudieron sostenerse como alternativa: el riesgo estaba en otra parte / "Animales imaginativos," nos decía Norman Brown, citando algo de Sade, de Vatsayana & riendo / La luna se les echó encima, viscosa / inesquivable, como si dejara el racionalismo olvidado bajo las llantas de un trailer allá por la constelación de Orión / Y la Angustia fue la única guerrilla urbana que reconocieron bajo estos cielos de manteca, hielo y smog no sólo síquicos. / En la calle, no en las bibliotecas, Rimbaud se aparecía con un conecte de visiones /

SECONDHAND HEROES:
SIX YOUNG MEXICAN INFRAREALISTS

For a sleepless art / against an opiate art
César Moro

I was going to thrash them within an inch of their lives,
but I didn't have a tape measure
Groucho Marx

To Groucho,
Chico & Harpo
so they feel
out of place

In 1968: less than 15 years old / watching gringo shows on T.V. / soldiers in the streets / flesh and blood communists agitating everywhere. Onward from there: living experience, living nightmare, living utopia / Emotion, sensation, the certainty of diving into chasms every moment transforming / Radical vagabonds, fugitives from the bourgeois university (the mediocrity of teaching is the teaching of mediocrity). They'd traveled highways, jungles, beaches where the Hon. Department of Tourism was trawling for at least some sickly "underground" / & they gassed & beat them, & they held their fists in the air, joking about LOSERS' POWER. Poetry (the rhetoric that went by that name) didn't involve them at all / Becerra, Pacheco couldn't stand as alternatives anymore: the risk was elsewhere / "Imaginative animals," Norman Brown said, citing some de Sade, Vatsayana & laughing / The moon was all over them, viscous / intrinsic, like it left rationalism for dead under the tires of a trailer out there in the Orion constellation / And Anguish was the only urban guerrilla they recognized under those skies of lard, ice, and smog that weren't only psychic. / In the street, not the libraries, Rimbaud appeared with a link to visions / in neighborhoods more crowded /

en los barrios más visitados que las viejas ermitas orientales, a la entrada de cines que los sofisticados llaman "de piojito" / Los borrachos los miraban con sus ojos de semáforo, como espejos tiznados donde se juntaran el mar rojo & el mar muerto / La Impaciencia se ponía a jugar tochito con los gorilitas más robustos de su lógica formal / Los poetas preciosistas hablaban de crepúsculos de metal, de cielos ardientes como ciruelas / y ellos leían los diarios / para conseguir un empleo / el menos feudal, el menos vampiro / Sus consignas: amor (al cubo) necesidad de otra cosa (a la enésima potencia) un resplandor llamado Whisky, una realidad inacabada, un sol con facha de radar, microscopio, ojo místico, espiándonos, radiotelegrafiándonos el derecho y el revés de cada escalofrío / Y así escaparon del dorado alacrán de la Costumbre y no los tocaron sus gordos aguaceros ni los enredaron sus alambres cloroformo / En la calle, no en las bibliotecas, bailaba la vida sus revelaciones más H20 / sus proporciones más desmelenadas & más sabias.

Deslícense en la vagina de una ballena viva / ¿Hay manera de hacer esto antes de 1985? Nam June Paik en una carta de John Cage.

Y en los jardines del Museo de Arte Moderno tú y yo nos besábamos, sudando, temblando, en la mejor jam-session de la contracultura, & Edvard Munch nos tomaba apuntes para un grabado, que de seguro llegaría a ser muy comercial & muy famoso / Delirios, fracturas, Tótem-realidad, Nuevas sensaciones que apuntan hacia Otra Naturaleza.

Se huelen días cálidos, llenos de sangre / There is a revolution going on in our skins: todavía puedo ver a Darío leyendo Auden, Lewis Carroll, Marqués de Sade, paseándose como la Divina de Genet por las azoteas, los subterráneos de la preparatoria 1; todavía se escapa del Neurológico, aprende a vivir la densidad de su experiencia marginal, siguiendo las huellas de bailarines terroristas hasta las playas de Zipolite, negándose a transar con la derecha gay; Mara Larrosa: militando en movimientos de liberación femenina: descubriendo la alquimia del cuerpo, las ingles de Nijinski, las posibilidades de una danza que va más allá de estos supermercados cavernícolas / primitiva, salvaje (roca transparente), mandándonos

than old oriental hermitages, in the lobbies of movie houses sophisticates call "fleabag" / Drunks looked on with their traffic light eyes like smudged mirrors where the red & the dead sea join / Impatience started playing touch football with the strongest little apes of its formal logic / The precious poets spoke of metal sunsets, skies blazing like plums / and read the newspapers / to get a job / the least feudal, the least vampiric / Their slogans: love (to the nth degree) another kind of need (to an exponential power) a radiance called Whisky, an incomplete reality, a sun that looked like radar, microscope, mystic eye, spying on us, radiotelegraphing us the inside and out of every shiver / And that's how they escaped the gilded scorpion of Custom and its swollen downpours didn't touch them and its chloroform wires didn't ensnare them / In the street, not the libraries, life danced its H20est revelations / its wisest & most unrestrained proportions.

Slide inside the vagina of a living whale / Is there some way to do this before 1985? Nam June Paik in a letter from John Cage.

And in the gardens of the Museum of Modern Art you & I kissed, sweating, trembling, in the counterculture's best jam session, & Edvard Munch took notes on us for an engraving that would of course become totally commercial & very famous / Deliriums, fractures, Totem-reality, New sensations pointing toward Another Nature.

You can smell the hot days coming, full of blood / There's a revolution going on in our skins: I can still see Darío reading Auden, Lewis Carroll, the Marquis de Sade, walking across rooftops, through the basement of public school 1 like the Divine Genet; still escaping from the Neurology Unit, learning to live the density of his marginal experience, following the footsteps of terrorist dancers to the beaches of Zipolite, refusing to compromise with the gay right; Mara Larrosa: fighting in women's liberation movements: discovering the body's alchemy, Nijinski's loins, the possibility of a dance that goes beyond those caveman supermarkets / primitive, savage (transparent rock), sending us a kiss from the background of an Albers painting, NO to Heartbreak. And Rubén plays on the harmonica and Peguero knocks on the door / & they don't let him in / & he throws a quarter at the window / & breaks it, dynamiting the eardrums of its nazi landlord.

un beso desde el fondo de una pintura de Albers, NO al Desamor. Y Rubén toca la armónica y Peguero la puerta / & no le abren / & tira un veinte contra la ventana / & la rompe, dinamitando los tímpanos de su casero nazi. Bajo las patas de una mesa del café La Habana, alfabetizando las caderas de grupies despistadas en los hoyos fonkies, inventando consignas personales en los mitines de Campa, mientras un ojo de Cuauhtémoc Méndez se carcajea con los chistes de Renato Leduc y el otro rueda por las calles colgado de la barbita que Revueltas y Bufalo Bill le envidiaron a León Trotski.

Lo que se había contenido se derrama / lo que no era visible pesa y se ve / toma un sabor de boca forzado / un sabor de sobaco, y de árbol / lo que era apenas voz hoy es voz, boca y saliva / Lo que no era nada ha vuelto.

La poesía mexicana deja de ser (queridito Villaurrutia) un anémico *nocturno en que nada se oye.*

Under the table legs at the Café Havana, instructing the hips of clueless groupies in funk dive bars, inventing private shibboleths at Campa*rallies while the eye of Cuauhtémoc Méndez laughs hysterically at Renato Leduc's jokes and the other guy rolls through the streets hanging by the Leon Trotsky goatee that José Revueltas and Buffalo Bill wished they had.

What was contained overflows / what was silenced speaks through arms and legs / what was unseen is visible and heavy / it takes the flavor of a mouth forced open / a flavor of armpits and trees / what was hardly a voice is now voice, mouth, and spit / What was nothing is back.

Mexican poetry stops being (my darling Villaurrutia) an anemic *nocturne in which nothing is heard.*

---

* Valentín Campa Salazar (1904–1999), labor activist, underground journalist, and the Mexican Communist Party's presidential candidate in 1976. Although the Party was not legally authorized to run a candidate, over 100,000 people attended the political meetings Campa held in support of academic freedom, workers' rights, democracy within the army, and other issues endorsed by various socialist organizations. Although the vote was never reported due to the unofficial nature of Campa's campaign, it is estimated that he received roughly one million votes.

MANIFIESTO INFRARREALISTA

¿QUÉ PROPONEMOS?
NO HACER UN OFICIO DEL ARTE
MOSTRAR QUE TODO ES ARTE Y QUE TODO MUNDO PUEDE HACERLO
OCUPARSE DE COSAS "INSIGNIFICANTES" / SIN VALOR INSTITUCIONAL / JUGAR / EL ARTE DEBE SER ILIMITADO EN CANTIDAD, ACCESIBLE
A TODOS, Y SI ES POSIBLE FABRICADO POR TODOS

!!!!!!!!!!!!!!!!!!!!!!!!!!!!!!!!!!!!

IMPUGNAR EL ARTE / IMPUGNAR LA VIDA COTIDIANA (DUCHAMP) EN UN TIEMPO QUE APARECE CASI ABSOLUTAMENTE BLOQUEADO PARA LOS
OPTIMISTAS PROFESIONALES
TRANSFORMAR EL ARTE / TRANSFORMAR LA VIDA COTIDIANA (NOSOTROS)
CREATIVIDAD / VIDA DESALINEADA A TODA COSTA
(MOVERLE LAS CADERAS AL PRESENTE CON LOS OJOS PESTAÑEANDO DESDE LOS AEROPUERTOS DEL FUTURO)
EN UN TIEMPO EN QUE A LOS ASESINATOS LOS HAN ESTADO DISFRAZANDO DE SUICIDIOS

$$$$$$$$$$$$$$$$$$$$$$$$$$$$$$$$$$$$$$$

CONVERTIR LAS SALAS DE CONFERENCIAS EN STANS DE TIRO
(FERIA DENTRO DE LA FERIA / ¿DIRÍA DEBRAY?)

%%%

INFRAREALIST MANIFESTO

WHAT DO WE PROPOSE?
NOT MAKING ART INTO A CAREER
SHOWING THAT EVERYTHING IS ART AND ANYONE CAN MAKE IT
CONCERNING OURSELVES WITH "INSIGNIFICANT" THINGS / WITH NO INSTIUTIONAL VALUE / PLAYING / ART SHOULD EXIST IN LIMITLESS AMOUNTS / AFFORDABLE
FOR EVERYONE, AND IF POSSIBLE, MADE BY EVERY-ONE

!!!!!!!!!!!!!!!!!!!!!!!!!!!!!!!!!!!!!!

ATTACKING ART / ATTACKING EVERYDAY LIFE (DUCHAMP) AT A TIME THAT SEEMS ALMOST ENTIRELY CLOSED TO PROFESSIONAL OPTIMISTS
TRANSFORMING ART / TRANSFORMING EVERYDAY LIFE (OURSELVES)
CREATIVITY / THE OUTSIDER'S LIFE AT ANY COST
(MOVING OUR HIPS TO THE PRESENT WITH EYES BLINKING FROM THE AIRPORTS OF THE FUTURE)
AT A TIME WHEN ASSASSINATIONS HAVE BEEN DISGUISED AS SUICIDES

$$

TURNING CONFERENCE ROOMS INTO SHOOTING GALLERIES
(THE CARNVIAL WITHIN THE CARNIVAL / AS DEBRAY WOULD PUT IT?)

%%

BEETHOVEN, RACINE & MIGUEL ÁNGEL DEJARON DE
SER LO MÁS ÚTIL
LO MÁS ANFETAMÍNICO, LO MÁS ALIMENTICIO:
LAS BARRERAS DEL SONIDO LOS LABERINTOS DE LA
VELOCIDAD (¡OH JAMES DEAN!) SE ESTÁN
ROMPIENDO EN OTRA PARTE

,,,

SACAR A LA GENTE DE SU DEPENDENCIA & PASIVIDAD
BUSCAR MEDIOS INÉDITOS DE INTERVENCIÓN & DE
DECISIÓN EN EL MUNDO
DESMITIFICAR / CONVERTIRSE EN AGITADORES
NADA HUMANO NOS ES AJENO (BIEN) NADA UTÓPICO
NOS ES AJENO (SUPERBIEN)

==================================

EN ESTA HORA MÁS QUE ANTERIORMENTE, EL PROBLEMA
ARTÍSTICO NO PUEDE SER CONSIDERADO COMO UNA
LUCHA INTERNA DE TENDENCIAS / SINO SOBRE TODO
COMO UNA LUCHA TÁCITA (CASI DECLARADA) ENTRE
QUIENES DE MANERA CONSCIENTE O NO ESTÁN CON EL
SISTEMA Y PRETENDEN CONSERVARLO PROLONGARLO /
Y QUIENES TAMBIÉN DE MANERA CONSCIENTE O NO
QUIEREN HACERLO ESTALLAR

• •

EL ARTE EN ESTE PAÍS NO HA IDO MÁS ALLÁ DE UN
CURSILLO TÉCNICO PARA EJERCER LA MEDIOCRIDAD
DECORATIVAMENTE

$$

"SOLAMENTE HOMBRES LIBRES DE TODA ATADURA

BEETHOVEN, RACINE & MICHAELANGELO AREN'T
THAT USEFUL ANYMORE
AMPHETAMINES MAKE BETTER FOOD:
SOUND BARRIERS LABYRINTHS OF SPEED (OH JAMES
DEAN!) ARE BEING BROKEN SOMEWHERE ELSE

,,,

LIFTING PEOPLE OUT OF THEIR DEPENDENCE &
PASSIVITY
LOOKING FOR UNPRECEDENTED FORMS OF
INTERVENTION & DIRECTION IN THE WORLD
DEMYSTIFYING / TURNING INTO DISSIDENTS
FOR US NOTHING HUMAN IS FOREIGN (COOL) FOR US
NOTHING UTOPIAN IS FOREIGN (SUPERCOOL)

===

NOW MORE THAN EVER, THE PROBLEM OF ART CAN'T
BE UNDERSTOOD AS AN INTERNAL WAR BETWEEN
FACTIONS / BUT ABOVE ALL AS A TACIT (BUT ALMOST
OPEN) WAR BETWEEN THE ONES WHO CONSCIOUSLY OR
UNCONSCIOUSLY SIDE WITH THE SYSTEM AND TRY TO
MAINTAIN AND EXTEND IT / AND THE ONES WHO
CONSCIOUSLY OR UNCONSCIOUSLY WANT TO BLOW IT UP

•••••••••••••••••••••••••••••••

ART IN THIS COUNTRY HASN'T GONE BEYOND A
TECHNICAL WORKSHOP FOR DECORATIVELY
EXERCIZING MEDIOCRITY

$$

"ONLY MEN FREE OF ALL BONDS CAN CARRY THE FIRE

PODRÁN LLEVAR EL FUEGO LO BASTANTE LEJOS" ANDRÉ
BRETON

!!

DEVOLVERLE AL ARTE LA NOCIÓN DE UNA VIDA
APASIONADA & CONVULSIVA

LA CULTURA NO ESTÁ EN LOS LIBROS NI EN LAS
PINTURAS NI EN LAS ESTATUAS ESTÁ EN LOS NERVIOS /
EN LA FLUIDEZ DE LOS NERVIOS
PROPOSICIÓN MÁS CLARA: UNA CULTURA ENCARNADA /
UNA CULTURA EN CARNE, EN SENSIBILIDAD (ESTE VIEJO
SUEÑO DE ANTONIN ARTAUD)

5555555555555555555555555555555555555555555555555555

TODO LO QUE EXISTE:
EL CAMPO DE NUESTRA ACTIVIDAD / Y LA BÚSQUEDA
FRENÉTICA DE LO QUE AÚN NO EXISTE

•••

NUESTRA FINALIDAD ES (LA VERDAD) LA SUBVERSIÓN
PRÁCTICA

&&&&&&&&&&&&&&&&&&&&&&&&&&&&&&&&&&&

EJEMPLO DE ARTE TOTAL
ESCULTURA TOTAL (Y CON MOVIMIENTO): UNA
MANIFESTACIÓN DE 10,000 A 20,000 GENTES APOYANDO
LA HUELGA DE LA TENDENCIA DEMOCRÁTICA DEL
SUTERM
MÚSICA TOTAL: UN VIAJE EN HONGO POR LA SIERRA
MAZATECA

FAR ENOUGH" ANDRÉ BRETON

!!!

RETURNING TO ART THE IDEA OF A CONVULSIVE &
PASSIONATE LIFE

CULTURE ISN'T IN BOOKS OR PAINTINGS OR STATUES
IT'S IN THE NERVES / IN THE NERVES' FLUIDNESS
THE CLEAREST PROPOSITION: AN INCARNATE CULTURE /
A CULTURE IN THE FLESH, IN SENSITIVITY (THE OLD
DREAM OF ANTONIN ARTAUD)

5555555555555555555555555555555555555555555555555

EVERYTHING THAT EXISTS:
OUR SPHERE OF ACTION / AND THE FRENZIED SEARCH
FOR WHAT DOESN'T EXIST YET

•••

OUR PURPOSE IS (TRUTH) PRACTICAL SUBVERSION

&&&&&&&&&&&&&&&&&&&&&&&&&&&&&&&&&&&

EXAMPLE OF TOTAL ART
TOTAL SCULPTURE (THAT MOVES): A DEMONSTRATION
OF 10,000 TO 20,000 PEOPLE SUPPORTING THE ELECTRICAL
WORKERS' UNION
TOTAL MUSIC: A MUSHROOM TRIP THROUGH THE
SIERRA MAZATECA

PINTURA TOTAL: CLAUDIA KERIK AL DERECHO & AL REVÉS / INSISTO: AL DERECHO & AL REVÉS

POESÍA TOTAL: ESTA ENTREVISTA DIFUNDIDA POR TELEPATÍA O CON EL SOLO MOVIMIENTO DE MI PELO (DE LEÓN AFRICANO) Y TODA SU DESCARGA ELÉCTRICA

33333333333333333333333333333333333333333333333

MUNDOS ONDAS GENTE QUE ME INTERESA:

NICANOR PARRA CATULO QUEVEDO LAUTRÉAMONT MAGRITTE CHIRICO ARTAUD VACHÉ JARRY BRETON BORIS VIAN BURRROUGHS GINSBERG KEROUAC KAFKA BAKUNIN CHAPLIN GODARD FASSBINDER ALAIN TANNER FRANCIS BACON DUBUFFET GEORGE SEGAL JUAN RAMÍREZ RUIZ VALLEJO EL CHÉ GUEVARA ENGELS "ESE MAESTRO DEL SARCASMO" LA COMUNA DE PARÍS LA INTERNACIONAL SITUACIONISTA LA EPOPEYA DE LOS NÁUFRAGOS DEL GRAMNA (SE ME OLVIDABA): HIERONYMUS BOSCH (EL INFALTABLE) WILHELM REICH LA PORNOGRAFÍA MÍSTICA DE CHARLES MAGNUS LA ERÓTICA MULTICOLOR DE TOM WESSELMAN JOHN CAGE JULIAN BECK JUDITH MALINA & SU LEAVING THEATRE (Y PARA FINALIZAR) EL MARQUÉS DE SADE HÉCTOR APOLINAR ROBERTO BOLAÑO JOSÉ REVUELTAS (Y SU DESCUBRIMIENTO DE QUE LA DIALÉCTICA A VECES TAMBIÉN ANDA COMO CANGREJO) JUDITH GARCÍA CLAUDIA SOL (Y HASTA EN DÍAS NUBLADOS) CLAUDIA SOL

%%%%%%%%%%%%%%%%%%%%%%%%%%%%%%%%%%%%%%%

PODEMOS DISPARAR 2 REVÓLVERES A LA VEZ / DIJO MÁS DE UNA VEZ BUFFALO BILL

LA ESTUPIDEZ NO ES NUESTRO FUERTE
(ALFRED JARRY DIXIT)

TOTAL PAINTING: CLAUDIA KERIK BACKWARDS &
FORWARDS / I INSIST: BACKWARDS AND FORWARDS
TOTAL POETRY: THAT INTERVIEW DISSEMINATED BY
TELEPATHY OR JUST THE FLICK OF MY (AFRICAN LION'S)
HAIR AND ITS FULL ELECTRICAL CHARGE

333333333333333333333333333333333333333333333

WORLDS MOVEMENTS PEOPLE THAT INTEREST ME:
NICANOR PARRA CATULLUS QUEVEDO LAUTRÉAMONT
MAGRITTE DE CHIRICO ARTAUD VACHÉ JARRY BRÉTON
BORIS VIAN BURROUGHS GINSBERG KEROUAC KAFKA
BAKUNIN CHAPLIN GODARD FASSBINDER ALAIN TANNER
FRANCIS BACON DUBUFFET GEORGE SEGAL JUAN
RAMÍREZ RUIZ VALLEJO CHÉ GUEVARA ENGELS "THAT
MASTER OF SARCASM" THE PARIS COMMUNE THE
SITUATIONIST INTERNATIONAL THE EPIC OF THE CUBAN
COMMUNIST PARTY'S SHIPWRECKS (I FORGOT):
HIERONYMUS BOSCH (ESSENTIAL) WILHELM REICH THE
MYSTICAL PORNOGRAPHY OF CHARLES MAGNUS THE
MULTICOLORED EROTICA OF TOM WESSELMAN JOHN
CAGE JULIAN BECK JUDITH MALINA & HER LIVING
THEATRE (AND FINALLY) THE MARQUIS DE SADE
HÉCTOR APOLINAR ROBERTO BOLAÑO JOSÉ REVUELTAS
(AND HIS DISCOVERY THAT DIALECTICS SOMETIMES
ALSO WALKS LIKE A CRAB) JUDITH GARCÍA CLAUDIA SOL
(AND EVEN ON CLOUDY DAYS) CLAUDIA SOL

%%

WE CAN SHOOT TWO REVOLVERS AT ONCE / SAID
BUFFALO BILL MORE THAN ONCE

STUPIDITY ISN'T OUR FORTE
(ALFRED JARRY DIXIT)

VISIÓN EN EL SINAÍ

Para Esther Cameo & Mauri Pilatowski

El vagabundo-ojos de iguana / pasó por aquí
& su sudor lo huelen todavía los vientos
los dioses-sangre de camello que habitan e iluminan el corazón de
    estas montañas
Las tribus de pastores de Beersheva
aún extrañan el canto lleno de ecos de sus botas
el fogonazo de su piel / tan parecida a 1 reata de muelle
con los mismos vaivenes de 1 salivazo de Arak
A la hora de los dátiles
los crepúsculos lentos / los fervorosos sorbos al jocoque
Agua noble le dicen en su dialecto los beduinos
& dibujan: 1 árbol con ropas colgando
        1 casa con alas en la arena
El vagabundo-ojos de iguana / pasó por aquí
& parecía 1 de esos rayos que escribían sin necesidad de olivettis-
    letteras & sin lápices
palabras capaces de dar cuerda al músculo azul de los patriarcas &
    sus pueblos
El vagabundo de lengua extrañísima
el cantador de cucurrucucús & ayayays
—al que seguían como a mancha de petróleo
los paracaidistas los radares israelíes—
El de las mejillas de cactus
el de los cigarros trepadores
el bebedor de escalofríos
el explorador de labios submarinos
el que se llevaba de *Salaam Aleko*
hasta con el seco vozarrón de las palmeras
El de la calaverita sonriente
grabada a punta de arañazos

VISION IN SINAI

For Esther Cameo & Mauri Pilatowski

The lizard-eyed tramp / passed through here once
& the winds & the gods with the blood of camels abiding in the
        heart of these mountains still smell his sweat
The shepherd tribes of Beersheba
still miss the echoing song of his boots
the flash of his skin / like cargo riggings
jiggling like 1 spitwad of arak
At the breaking of the fast
the slow coming of twilight / the fervent swigs of buttermilk
Noble water they say in their Bedouin dialect
& they draw: 1 tree draped with clothes
                1 winged house in the sand
The lizard-eyed tramp / passed through here once
& was like 1 of those lightning bolts that wrote with no need for
        pencils or portable typewriters
words to oblige the blue muscle of the patriarchs & their peoples
The wild-tongued tramp
singing *cucurrucucús & ayayays*
—who Israeli radar & paratroopers
followed like 1 oil stain—
The 1 with the cheeks of 1 cactus
the 1 with the vine-like cigars
the 1 who drank human fear
the explorer of deep sea lips
the 1 whose *Salaam Aleko* appeased
even the thundering voice of the palms
The 1 with the smiling little skull
etched by claw

en el hueso-vida perpetua de su mochila de viaje
Él / que besaba la rarísima llegada de las lluvias
& se abría como sólo la tierra pocas veces
& se abría / como si en ese momento todos nos fuéramos a morir

in the eternal bone-life of his rucksack
He / who kissed the precious coming of the rain
& opened himself as only the earth rarely does
& opened himself / as if at that moment we were all marching off
        to die

YA LEJOS DE LA CARRETERA

A la memoria de Infraín

> *Vibraciones*
> *vibraciones-látigo*
> *1 sonido viene de la sombra*
> *pronto forma 1 esfera :*
> *1 granja :*
> *1 grupo :*
> *1 armada :*
> *1 universo de universos*
> Henri Michaux

1

Unos pantalones mugrosos & la muerte en el pecho
¡Órale!
Nos vemos ahí en el muro
/ pasando el vado /
los vientos cristalizándose a la izquierda
las aletas del polvo : tus aletas
1 oasis arponeándonos lo seco
En la hija de tu ojo / el cementerio
: Mezcalito echando flores :
La Tierra & su contrario : venados silenciosos como ruidos en sus bodas
No deberías ir / pero deberías ir

2

(En esta sombra se acurruca esta rara fruta
que es el corazón anfibio & precoz devenir infrarrealista)
    Hijos de Pablo de Rokha somos
Desde antes de escribir esto / ya volábamos
Luego el continuum de lo escrito fue menos vigilado

ALREADY FAR FROM THE ROAD

To the memory of Infrain

Vibrations
Vibrations-whips
1 sound comes from the shadow
quickly forms 1 sphere :
1 farm :
1 group :
1 armada :
1 universe of universes
Henri Michaux

1

Some grubby pants & death in the chest
        Right on man!
I'll see you there by the wall
/ just past the loading zone /
winds crystallizing on the left
fins of the dust : your fins
1 oasis harpooning the dryness in us
In the daughter of your eye / the graveyard
 : Mezcalito casting posies :
Earth & its opposite : deer silent as the noises at their weddings
You shouldn't go / but you should go

2

(In this shadow this strange fruit nestles that's the heart
of the amphibious & precocious infrarealist becoming)
   Sons of Pablo de Rokha are we
Before writing this / we were already flying
Then the continuum of the written was less patrolled

Bailó el aliento en la punta de la lengua
Nos transfiguramos acariciando el ayayay de cada llaga

> *Somos poetas*
> *Tam-tams del negro sol*
> *que nos imanta*

3

Ni lúmpenes ni proletarios
El pequeñodios cobrasalarios
ni 1 pluma rompe en los abismos nuestros
: Las auroras infras en la Casa de Usher de la araña :
Juega al balero el dulce clítoris / se embarca como a las 5
       montañas en 2 cuatros
A galope tierno & crines sueltas
    Rubayat ama
        a
    Ramayana

4

Nuestra lengua ha sido púa
Es sandía / chorreante vagabunda de ancha risa
Aventura que nos ha abierto escoriaciones
Lo que éramos lo somos en el crescendo de los ecos
    A tales hombros : tales caderas
    A esos tobillos / aquellos pasos
El aprendizaje de la limpieza al escalpelo

Breath danced on the tip of the tongue
We transformed caressing the ayayay of every wound

We're poets
Cymbals of the black sun
that magnetizes us

3

Neither lumpens nor proletarians
The wage-earning demigod
not 1 pen bursts in our abysses
: The infra-dawns in the spider's House of Usher :
Sweet clitoris plays paddle ball / embarks as for the 5 mountains in
        2 lutes
At tender gallop & flowing mane
        Rubayat is in love
                with
        Ramayana

4

Our tongue has been barbed
It's watermelon / dripping deep-laughing vagrant
Adventure that's torn open our abrasions
What we've been we are in the crescendoing of echoes
        For such shoulders : such thighs
        For those ankles / those steps
Lessons of cleansing by the scalpel

5

...Gris es la Teoría...
Rojo el vellón de la Cannabis / la Inalámbrica

6

¿La lucha? / Contra el poder de $igno$ fari$aico$
(Máscara *vs* Cabellera)
10 años después seguimos siendo Tribu
/ dondequiera lúbricos /
En Jalalpa : Minneapolis : Iquitos : Ivre Sur de Seine : Gerona :
el Barranco & la Cañada
Perros habitados por las voces del desierto
Tlamatinimes obcecados por la flama del canto por el cuerpo
& la flama del cuerpo que es el canto
¡Tlacoyos de realidad!

7

El rastrojo del lenguaje no germina
si no es en hechos menguaje ya encarnado
La hazaña marabusina en tierras nahuas
—¿De a cómo la liebre lírica? / ¿con alas?
—Feliz No-Cumpleaños
El infrarrealismo no es 1 vocablo-lija
Nos han antologado nuestras noches
Cada textículo en su sitio / que bien puede ser nuestro milagro
nómada

5

...Gray is the Theory...
Red the fuzz of Cannabis / The Wireless

6

The fight? / Against the power of phara$aical ign
             (Mask *vs* Longhair)
10 years later we're still being tribal
             / lubricous wherever /
In Jalapa : Minneapolis : Iquitos : Ivry-sur-Seine : Gerona :
             Glen & Canyon
Dogs inhabited by voices of the desert
Aztec priests blinded by the flame by the song of the body
& the flame of the body that's the song
             Reality sandwiches!

7

The compost of language doesn't germinate
if it isn't in deeds already poverty incarnate
The Marabu triumph in Nahuatl lands
—How much for the singing rabbit? / With wings?
—Happy Un-Birthday
Infrarealism isn't some scouring-word
Our nights have anthologized us
Every texticle in its place / that could likely be our nomad's miracle

8.

Es Hora Zero otra vez
Jesús Luis rasga en su luz *Canciones para gandallas*
Hay estrellas como hay ganas
hay abismos & hay caminos
Las pirañas de anteayer
son iguanas a futuro
Olas : olas : olas de sed

9

—¿Qué decían de nosotros esos empleados televisivos?
/ hijos del feliz oficio & el próspero cheque de honorarios /
—Oh Santas Risas Satánicas
—¿Ni Billy Burroughs lo sabe?
        El petate da de brincos
        / Son cocuyos en la aurora /
—¿Será eso 1 hai-kai sirio?
¿1 poeta náutico en la sierra?
¿El orgasmo del delirio?

10

Poesía-endecasilabóiler
    hermanita de Edgar Allan & Black Sabbath
        caradiajos & chintreras
            qué de arrastres
                labrados en la entraña de la entraña

8

It's Zero Hour again
Jesús Luis scratches *Songs for Thugs* in its light
There are stars like there are desires
there are abysses & there are roads
The piranhas of the day before yesterday
are iguanas of the future
Waves : waves : waves of thirst

9

—What'd those TV employees say about us?
/ sons of happy service & generous benefits /
—Oh Holy Satanic Laughter
—Billy Burroughs doesn't even know?
          The bedroll jumps for joy
          / They're fireflies at dawn /
—Is that 1 Syrian haiku?
1 water poet in the sierras?
Delirium's orgasm?

10

Poetry-hendecasyllaboiler
   Edgar Allan & Black Sabbath's little sister
      dickfaces & fucktrarians
         so many trenches
            plowed in the guts of the guts

11

Toco viento
: azar turgente:
Nuestra raíz está hablando
/ no el enjuague del Poder & sus taquillas
sus tarifas : sus castigos : muecas cínicas : su estertor de vanidades /

12

Que Tin-Tan queme su saco
Los caminos están llenos de otros seres
        / no el cubículo ni el cargo /
Recuerda cuerpo cuanto viviste
    Cuánto evangelio de cielos abiertos
      / Subterráneamente : soberanamente /
Porque no será el miedo a ningún miedo
el que nos haga poner a media asta
el géiser ígneo de nuestra indignación

& este número 13 bien lo dice:
La poesía mexicana se divide en 2
la poesía mexicana & el infrarrealismo
    / Río Tula a remover /

11
        I touch wind
: turgid chance :
Our root is talking
/ not the laundering of Power & its ticket-booths
its taxes : its punishments : cynical grins : its wheezing of vanities /

12
Let Tin-Tan burn his zoot suit
The roads are full of other beings
        / not the cubicle or charge /
Remember body how much you lived
    How much gospel of the open heavens
        / Subterraneously : sovereignly /
Because it won't be the fear of any fear
that makes us set at half mast
the igneous geyser of our indignation

& this numeral 13 says it well:
Mexican poetry is divided in 2
Mexican poetry & infrarealism
    / 1 Tula River to stir up /

El asesino sonámbulo cruzó los portales de la pesadilla vacía
Nevaba en la azorada noche de abril
La huelga de basura había llegado a sus sienes
Apretaba el héroe su abrigo escarlata chorreado de esperma
La excitación le besaba los pies
Las botas / el olor a 1 destino presentido en fulgurantes viajes de chemo
¡Aaarrrgggghhh!
La leona parisina paría 1 cagarruta más de leyenda & de tedio
Pero la sed / el irresistible imán del deseo de más miel encendida /
empujaba a nuestro Lord Jim Catacumbas a arrancarse las barbas
a correr persiguiendo el coño de 1 ángel que sólo a él le huía
((De Chirico observaba como ojo de torre brotado sin reglas))
El asesino sonámbulo se sentó sobre el puente volado del Metro
        Passy
El frío le abría las entrañas / la atarjea que unía la caída de 1 sueño
al torrente imparable de otro *speed* de *haschisch*
Esa noche la Comuna era masacrada para todos los tiempos
El burdel se pudría con singular sinsentido
¡Lo más lejos del río! : garabateó afónico lo que quedaba de instinto
El asesino / desnudo / ensayaba piruetas
arrastrando a tajadas los carámbanos manchados de su abrigo-bandera
Su navaja era el cielo que renunciaba a ser cielo
La nieve : la víctima
1 crucifixión sin raíces poblaba los vagones suspendidos
en la memoria del *clochard* revoltoso que asaltaba esa noche
la historia perdida del Metro Passy
Tachadas la *pe* / la *a* / la doble *ese* / la *y* griega
con golpes de vidrio la estación fue bautizada como Metro Landrú
1 botellazo de *Viuda* / 2 oraciones en turco

The sleepwalking assassin passed the gates of empty nightmare
It was snowing in the flustered April night
The garbage strike had reached his forehead
The hero was clutching his sperm-drenched scarlet coat
Excitement kissed his feet
His boots / the scent of 1 destiny foretold on luminous glue trips
Aaarrrggghhh!
The Parisian lioness was giving birth to 1 more turd of tedium & myth
But the thirst / the irresistible magnet of desire for more burning honey /
drove our Lord Jim of the Catacombs to tear out his beard
to run after the cunt of 1 angel who only fled from him
((De Chirico looked on like the eye of 1 irregularly sprouted tower))
The sleepwalking assassin sat on the blown-up bridge of the Metro
Passy
Cold tore through his guts / the sewer line linking the fall in 1 dream
to the unstoppable torrent of another speed of hash
The Commune was massacred once & for all that night
The brothel rotted with exceptional futility
As far away from the river! : What was left of instinct mutely scrawled
The assassin / naked / attempted pirouettes
dragging the dirty icicle shreds of his coat-flag
His knife was the sky that renounced being sky
The snow : the victim
1 rootless crucifixion peopled the wagons suspended
in the memory of the rebel clochard who raided the lost history
of the Metro Passy that night
scratched out the *p* / the *a* / the double *s* / the *y*
baptized the station the Metro Landrú with blows of glass
1 bottle of sangria to the head / 2 prayers in Turkish

: Mi palacio es de vértebras / mi río Sena de orín :
     Ya sin aspas el mundo
     En santa paz la carroña
Hiperebrio el silencio : amamantando las grietas de 1 mítica Anexas

: My palace is of vertebrae / my River Seine of piss :
    The world now propellerless
    Carrion in holy peace
Silence drunk off its ass : suckling the cracks of 1 mythic annexation

ESTOY SANGRANDO POR LOS 5 SENTIDOS

El escudo del sol se deja herir por 1 lluvia de piernas
Pasa 1 cisne fumando
Las taquimecanógrafas se retiran del Sena
rumbo a Nanterre
Sólo los clochards hieren / consumen & vuelven a herir
lo que queda & sigue quedando de los sudores del Gólgota
Qué diferencia hay entre romperse & cantar
Llueve / es cierto /
& las bailarinas
   & los arponeros no duermen
¿El control policial
       terminará ahogado en el vino?
¿Alá / Dionysos / Caupolicán / Ratatá?
1 niño árabe rasga la inmovilidad de unos dados
sopla: baila: dispara
su sonrisa morena
ya torció los alambres-carne molida
del nerviosísimo cielo
/ ¿Verdad Márgara? /
La Gorda Sombra está sembrando castaños
1 retablo de jugos sexuales le pide aventón a 1 poeta
(((que ha comenzado a alucinar hacia atrás)))
El sol mejor se sienta en lo más alto de 1 beso
   —& para qué pestañas / cachuchas—
Voltaire da de vueltas
      con 1 rehilete de niños
Rabelais no critica: destruye
La Bardot ha adoptado a mis piojos
Raro censo
El Sena lo firma
    & se hecha 1 bucito
Animal herido de muerte

I'M BLEEDING FROM ALL 5 SENSES

The shield of the sun is wounded by 1 rain of legs
1 swan passes by smoking
Stenographers withdraw from the Seine
in the direction of Nanterre
Only thieves wound / consume & go back to wounding
what remains & keeps remaining of Golgotha's sweat
What's the difference between shattering yourself & singing
Rain / is certain /
& the dancers
        & harpooners can't sleep
Will police control
            end up drowned in wine?
Allah / Dionysus / Caupolicán / Ratatá?
1 Arab boy breaks the stillness of 1 pair of dice
blows: dances: shoots
his tawny smile
already torqued the ground beef tripwires
of hyper-nervous heaven
/ Right Márgara? /
The Fat Shadow is planting chestnuts
1 altar of sexual juices bums 1 ride from 1 poet
(((who has started hallucinating backwards)))
The sun sits best on the peak of 1 kiss
    —& for what eyelashes / what caps—
Voltaire runs around & around
            with 1 pinwheel
Rabelais doesn't criticize: he destroys
Brigitte Bardot has adopted my lice
Strange survey
The Seine signs it
        & goes for 1 dip
Fatally wounded beast

((ha dejado 1 recado))
Sin tintas / cedazos o hamacas
Sin angustias / arañazos o hendiduras de mono
Reculando bien firme
Chilleteando bien hondo
Sencillamente
A lo sincho
A lo breve
Cabeza de piedra entregada al delirio
(Sin verdugos / madrinas o paros)
El paisaje se ha puesto a bailar Ricachá

((it left 1 message))
Without inks / strainers or slings
Without anguish / gashes or claw marks
Retreating steadily
Whining deeply
Simply
Straight up
Short and sweet
1 stone head driven to madness
(Without hangmen / godmothers or shutdowns
The landscape starts dancing the Cha-Cha-Chá

RETRATO DE MEMORIA DE MI PADRE JACK KEROUAC / DESDE ESTA ESTACIÓN DEL UNIVERSO

Sus aletas de delfín no son voluminosas ni visibles
pero qué vuelo de arpón el de su risa
& cómo rompe termómetros su llanto
Si el mar : su irrenunciable mar
pierde carne / carne & uñas
la carretera-garganta sin fin de sus húmedos instintos
emborracha con la dulzura
con la que 1 niño aprieta explora
bautiza por primera vez su nebulosa
Desnudez que llueve truena rehiletea olas
reinventando lo que antes sólo se llamaba
labio o sólo beso o sólo viento
viento de viento / trabalenguas que se pellizcaba solo
Sin 1 solo salto sorpresa
en el radar o en la brújula encharcada
de este ser balsa & fauno
nervio & cosquilla remanervios
Contagioso-íntegro-febril acercapájaros
al que yo le dedico—entre destellos—
estos rayos de luz-bragueta abierta
la escultura de amor
yegua ardiente de jadeos
Ángel subterráneo
que hace sudar al pacto interno que frota esta canción

PORTRAIT FROM MEMORY OF MY FATHER JACK KEROUAC / FROM THIS STATION OF THE UNIVERSE

Your dolphin fins aren't voluminous or visible
but your laughter—what thrust of the harpoon
& how your moans break thermometers
If the sea : your inalienable sea
loses its flesh / flesh & fingernails
the endless highway-throat of its damp instincts
gets drunk with the sweetness
of 1 boy squeezing exploring
baptizing his nebula for the first time
Nakedness that rains thunders churns up waves
reinventing what before was just called
lips or just kisses or just wind
the wind of wind / tongue-twisters he only had to pinch
Without even 1 unexpected surge
on the radar or the waterlogged compass
of this raft & fawn being
nerve & nerve-racking tickle
Contagious-complete-feverish birdwatcher
to whom I dedicate—between flashes—
these rays of light with their fly down
the sculpture of love
the burning mare of gasps
Subterranean angel
making the private covenant this song caresses break out in sweat

CORRESPONDENCIA INFRA

El mar toca nuestros cuerpos
para sentir su cuerpo
Lo mismo en Manzanillo pedregoso
que en Neviot / isla de corales del desierto
Nosotros devolvemos su sonrisa de sal
dibujando nuestros nombres & apetencias
en el caparazón de los cangrejos
que parecen buscar viejas patas de palo devoradas por la arena
El mar se para de cabeza
& nos canta / en el idioma más desnudo & afín a nuestro tacto
Port Vendrés Ville ruge como atún encolerizado en nuestros ojos
Bernard prende 1 de sus aretes verde flúor en la cabellera alfilereada
        de 1 erizo
Los demás pescadores del *Saint Joan / Fetiche II*
desde sus camarotes se sinceran a su modo
con éste también su mar que los filma fijamente
Ahí donde ellos se aflojan su nervioso pantalón
& sus labios no dejan de ulular
cuando ven hasta las anginas del Peñón de Gibraltar
moviéndose como dados o peces plateados
en la sombra de sus vasos de ron

INFRA CORRESPONDENCE

The sea touches our bodies
to feel its body
The same in rocky Manzanillo
as in Neviot / coral island of the desert
We return its salten smile
sketching our names & cravings
on the shells of crabs
that seem to be hunting for wooden legs swallowed by the sand
The sea stands on its head
& sings to us / in the naked language most kindred to our touch
Port-Vendres Ville rages like 1 angry tuna in our eyes
Bernard hangs 1 of his green fluoride earrings in the spiny hair
       of 1 sea urchin
The other fishermen of the *Saint Joan / Fetish II*
come clean their own way in their cabins
with this 1 this sea of theirs steadily filming them
There where they loosen their nervous trousers
& their ululating lips don't stop
when they see to the tonsils of the Rock of Gibraltar
shaking like dice or silvery fish
in the shadow of their glasses of rum

ABISINIA'S SHOCK

¡1 carga de oro para el aguilucho Rimbaud!
150 táleros : pieza x pieza :
¿Qué querrá decir este viento de aves / anestesiada la tarde?
Tanta vagancia & pasión ¿qué querrán decir?
Este texto brotado del túnel ansía dibujarlo
:: Adolescente espectral / feto prodigio
Camellero del limbo / Negación & vaivén ::
Sí, el poeta es realmente 1 ladrón de fuego
¿Qué ha pasado ¡carajo! del *Vuelve, vuelve Verlaine*
                    al marfil / las caravanas / la costa?
Los fantasiosos los bohemios los talentos los muertos
& los imbéciles le calentaron la videncia hasta el mástil
            & el ángel se largó a reencontrarse
            ((& se arrojó de lleno))
            Ayer / si mal no recuerdo

ABYSSINIA'S SHOCK

1 shipment of gold for the eaglet Rimbaud!
150 thalers : piece x piece :
What could this wind of birds mean / in the anesthetized evening?
So much vagrancy & passion / what could they mean?
This text sprung from the tunnel yearns to depict it
:: Spectral adolescent / prodigious fetus
Camel driver of limbo / Negation & vacillation ::
Yes, the poet really is 1 thief of fire
What the fuck happened to *Come back, come back Verlaine*
            to the ivory / the caravans / the coast?
The dreamers the bohemians the talents the dead
& the imbeciles kindled his clairvoyance to the topmast
        & the angel went off to find him again
        ((& plunged all the way in))
        Yesterday / if memory serves

HIJOS DEL REY LOPITOS

Nuestra aventura fue ésta:
—otro rayo en las bragas del caos—
Despertar / sumergirnos
Como ola la piel estrellada
En contextos no siempre reales
En los techos de Circe
—bugambilia fogosa—
el cristal de los cantos fue la forja
el afán / la escritura de días en océanos nublados
/ Cosmoalfiles /
Sex Raza
Elegimos el licor del insomnio al s*peech* de la zarza
En playas de dunas
Bajo el coral que amaranta
& recordamos 1 prisma / 1 botón de mujer
en los hoteles del alba
Otra vez ruede & ruede
Experiencia flamígera / girasol de cascadas
El fulgor de los bosques
los *highways* sensoriales
Meteoritos de angustia
salpicando sus péndulos / tierra ardida / quema de llantas
Es 1 diapasón de la tribu
este gajo de luz en los dedos / la bacha / de la bacha más brava
En la ronda los cuates se transfiguraron carnales
No fue caspa del tiempo
Fue soñar otras danzas
El Watusi & el Chivo presumiendo de báquicos
El hotpant de la ninfa
/ le respondí a Vasconcelos /
Navegamos quemando
En la grieta: las plantas las enredaderas nerviosas

THE SONS OF KING LOPITOS*

Our adventure was this:
—another lightning bolt in the panties of chaos—
To wake up / to immerse ourselves
Like 1 wave the starry skin
In contexts not always real
On Circe's rooftops
—fiery bougainvillea—
the crystal of the Cantos was the forge
the drive / the writing of days on cloudy oceans
/ Cosmobishops /
Sex Aztecs
We chose the liquor of insomnia over the speech of the burning bush
On dune beaches
Under amaranthine coral
& remembered 1 prism / 1 woman's button
in the hotels of dawn
Roll & roll again
Flaming experience / sunflower waterfalls
Forests' radiance
Sensory highways
Meteors of anguish
splattering their tails / scorched earth / burnt rubber
It's 1 pitch pipe of the tribe
this wedge of light between fingers / the roach / of the fiercest blunt
In this circle pals became brothers
It wasn't the dandruff of time
It was dreaming other dances
The Watusi & the Chivo trumped up as bacchanals
The nymph's hot-pants
/ I replied to Vasconcelos /
Burning we steered
Through the cleft: the plants the anxious climbing vines

el nocturno acné que mandrilean las luciérnagas
El avispero del rol
En los barrios del perro chamán & la perra yerbera
& los hijos: hipnosis / hidalgos del puño del polvo
frotando el sol de su ruta
arenas abajo del viento / del diente / del sólido mar
Abluciones de escándalo
Los nudillos golpeando
La cantata ceñida al carril que trotamos
Cantarando & bailando
((la seda en la raya))
siemprevivas eternas
al sagrado & luminoso coito del bifronte amor
Sin importarnos chile piquín orégano estertores ocotes o precio

the nocturnal acne that fireflies drill
The hornet's nest of sleep
In the barrios of the shaman dog & the herbalist bitch
& their sons: hypnosis / knights of the fistful of dust
rubbing the sun from its path
sands beneath the wind / the tooth / of solid sea
Scandalous ablutions
Knuckles striking
The cantata tied to the tracks we walked
Incanting & dancing
((like silk on the line))
eternal live-forevers
to the sacred & luminous coitus of 2-faced love
Without caring 1 chile piquín oregano sprig death rattles pine tree
       or price

* Alfredo López Cisneros (1923–1966), commonly known as "Rey Lopitos" [King Lopitos], led the popular land reclamation movement in Acapulco during the 1950s and 1960s.

CAMINO A TEOTITLÁN DEL CAMINO
PERO AÚN EN EL METRO SAN LÁZARO

Chueco de risa ((rebotando))
Oloroso / casi a punto
Con mi uñas de zancudo
exprimiéndole en lo más hondo su sinrazón al agua
Por los hornos de la lluvia me remojo
No retrato / no mastico / no interrumpo
el romance indio & denso de mis choclos con los charcos
Salto en frío
Estas calles de mis fórceps:
estas idas y venidas de mis años desempleados
          me vacilan / me rasuran
Ni 1 orgasmo me han ahogado
Sin aletas ni escafandra sobrevivo
& hasta escribo—entre los peces—
& he aprendido trompetillas
& a rascarme suspirando
No precisamente a ras del musgo
/ ni lejanamente sepultado /

I WALK TO TEOTITLÁN DEL CAMINO
EVEN ON THE METRO SAN LÁZARO

Distorted grin ((rebounding))
Aromatic / almost ready
Squeezing the illogic of water from its very depths
with my pincers
I bathe in furnaces of rain
I don't portray / I don't contemplate / I don't interrupt
the thick & Indian romance of the puddles with my boots
Like it's nothing I leap
These streets of my forceps:
these comings & goings of my destitute years
          shake me up / shave me down
They haven't drowned even 1 of my orgasms
Without flippers or 1 diving suit I survive
& even write—among the fish—
& I've learned the ear trumpet
& to scratch myself by sighing
Not exactly at the level of the moss
/ but not buried far off /

DEUX MACHINA
/ EN LAS AFUERAS
((CADA VEZ MÁS AFUERA))
DE LA ESTACIÓN DEL METRO BELÉN /

Para Mowgli

Ya vienen los Reyes
& vienen repránganas
Ya vienen los Reyes
Los Reyes del Reven
Revirados los sueños
Los vuelos colgando del peciolo de 1 precio
Stripers: travestis: jornaleros sudados / estos Reyes sin redes
Su trapecio es 1 hacha que obedece a su pálpito
Polvaredas de ciudades perdidas
Cagada fresca / junto al manantial /
Husmeadores del rocío perineal que decide la erección de 1 estrella
No está en oferta vivir a extramuros
Esta noche no hay neón no manchado
Los pastores pepenan calambres
Sus mujeres se masturban frente al control remoto de sus ciegas tevés
Huele a thinner & a elote quemado
A la celda le están despintando su cielo
El hombre invisible de mi Dios Julio Verne
no me sirve hoy para robar & crecer
Las multitudes estorban el milagro de besar el suave labio nacido
Pronta su risa / disuelve peligros
: desbarata acertijos :
Que el oro / la mirra / el incienso
se lo sorban los torvos tragones de las superficie
Hay campanas internas
/ más allá del eructo del cláxon
& el mudo mundo del loco motor /

DEUS EX MACHINA
/ ON THE PERIPHERY
((INCREASINGLY PERIPHERAL))
OF THE BETHLEHEM METRO STATION /

For Mowgli

Here come the Kings
& they come empty-handed
Here come the Kings
The Comeback Kings
Dreams contorted
Wings hanging by the petiole of 1 pricetag
Strippers: transvestites: sweaty workmen / these Kings without nets
Their trapeze is 1 axe that follows its hunch
Dust clouds of lost cities
Fresh shit / next to the wellspring /
Huffers of the perineal dew that dictates the erection of 1 star
Living outside the city walls isn't on sale
No neon tonight is unstained
Shepherds pick over cramps
Their wives masturbate in front of their blind TVs' remote controls
It smells like paint thinner & burnt corn
They're stripping the jail cell's sky
The invisible man of my God Jules Verne
doesn't help me to steal & to flourish today
Crowds block the miracle of kissing the soft-born lip
Their ready laugh / dissolves dangers
: destroys riddles :
That gold / myrrh / incense
is slurped from the surface by brooding gluttons
There are internal bells
/ beyond the car horn's belch
& the mad engine's mute world /

A pincel & cantando
A patín de pezuña
Arrastrando los callos
Con el bofe en la mano
La integridad sin rajarse
Ahí vienen los Reyes
Bien firmes
Bien tómbolas
Sólo basta con verlos
galopar en la piel de la luna
: los bolsillos rotísimos
todo el cuerpo tatuado :
Persiguiendo el impulso
—su loco deseo—
de tirarse clavados
/ sin trampolín de por medio /
Hasta el fondo del fondo del mar

Painted & singing
Skating on hooves
Scraping off calluses
Your guts in your hand
Unboasting integrity
Now here come the Kings
Steadily
By lottery
It's enough just to see them
gallop in the skin of the moon
: their pockets in tatters
their whole bodies tattooed :
Chasing the impulse
—their crazy desire—
to hurl themselves nailed
/ without 1 trampoline beneath /
To the bottom of the ocean floor

CLARIDAD BIZARRA

Para Laura Barcia

descubro el mundo
en los espejos
que rompo
con mis diferencias
Cioran / en 1 sueño

la raza está demente
pero a punta de miserias
des(h)ojada
Ricardo Flores Magón / en otro sueño

Fíjate que no importa si abrazas
  1 labio de sol o 1 semáforo
  1 alarma contra robos
    o 1 lluvia nacida de las piedras
Hablar sin tripas
  respirar con los gramos despintados
    graduarse por larga duración
      en las heráldicas cojeantes de la especie
es ahora boleto / vale de descuento
  binocular maquillaojos
    peine tenido por espátula escultórica
      spray-mil usos / condón usado hasta de macarrón & de manguera
      cuerda para saltar, banda presidencial
        collar para el moquillo, pilar de oro & plata
          que decora las caricaturas de *Himeneo*
Las bellezas evidentes jadean pegadazas a los idiotas doctorados
Poesía llega hasta en auxilio de sus enemigos
Kaos le aclara a *Orden* el uso fertilizante de sus fantasmagóricas
    diarreas

BIZARRE CLARITY

For Laura Barcia

I discover the world
in the mirrors
I break
with my difference
Cioran / in 1 dream

the race is demented
but on the point of destitution
decapitated
Ricardo Flores Magón / in another dream

See it doesn't matter if you embrace
  1 lip of sun or 1 traffic light
  1 burglar alarm
    or rain sprung from 1 stone
To speak with no guts
  to breathe with the grams rubbed off
    to graduate by long duration
      into the heraldic limpings of the species
now it's 1 ticket / discount voucher
  binocular eye makeup
    dye job by sculptor's spatula
      multipurpose spray / condom used even for macaroni or 1 hose
        jump rope, presidential ribbon
          dog collar for distemper, pillar of gold & silver
          adorning the caricatures of *Hymen*
The evident beauties stuck to the idiot PhDs are panting
  Poetry even comes to the aid of its enemies
  Kaos clarifies for *Order* the fertilizing use of its phantasmagoric
      diarrhea

Andamos fritos / & se nos clasifica
  como irremplazables conductores
    de 1 "supuesto" cortocircuito "hipotéticamente"
           vacilador/ tonificante
& resulta que los monstruos
    somos espectáculo / aquarimántima ambulante
        locos cómplices
Hay lugar spichean los tecnócratas
No hay ni 1 alma es el grito del último cisne
          herido de castrati
El albañil que se cae del andamio & ya no almuerza
el guerrillero que se pudre de dolor inmóvil & dinamiterísima
    impotencia
son en el cuarto oscuro de este código-cámara de gases
  imágenes que se filman & se cuentan
    medallas agradables
      a las que guiñando el ojo
        se les pide en buena mímica el engorde de la suerte
        El sudor de los desesperados
        se embotella en tetrapack
        o se tira a la basura
a la basura misma se le hace que se apode
la basura misma ejemplarísimo pesebre

En las escuelas / & horas más tarde en los estadios
  a las bombas de tiempo
    resulta que les llamas
      balones con hexágonos
El lenguaje avorázado del ozono
  la delicia chupachupa de la vida
    la sodomía aprietamares
      que hizo a esta tierra contemplar
        dinosaurios de pasión
          regadereándose en espermas-rayosláser
            que brotaban brincoteando / de la herida

We're wasted / & they classify us
  as irreplaceable conductors
    of 1 "so-called" short circuit "hypothetically"
                comical / refreshing
& it turns out we monsters
are the show / *acuarimántima** embodied
              crazy accomplices
There is 1 place the technocrats speechify
There's not even 1 soul is the scream of the last
                   castrated swan
The bricklayer who falls from the scaffold & no longer eats lunch
the soldier who rots in motionless pain & explosive impotence
  are images that chronicle & film themselves
   in the darkroom of this gas chamber-camera
    trophies that amuse
      those skillful mimes who ask them with 1 wink
        to fatten up their luck
        The sweat of the desperate
        is bottled in tetrapacks
        or thrown in the garbage
& as for the garbage itself they make it go by the nickname
the garbage itself exemplary trough

In schools / & hours later in stadiums
  it turns out you call
   time bombs
    balls with hexagons
The avaricious language of the ozone
  the sucksuck delight of life
   the sea-squeezing sodomy
    that made this earth contemplate
     dinosaurs of passion
      hosing themselves down with laserbeam-sperm
       that came shooting forth / from the volcanos'

      más esencial a los volcanes
      YA NO EXISTE
Imaginación amaba entonces
 respetando muy en serio el natural copilotaje de la Muerte
   Imaginación amaba entonces
    & ese juego importaba / paría aires
    & si no los paría
    ni pretextando el influjo de los sismos los mataba
      IMAGINACIÓN AMABA
      ENTONCES/ Sí Sí Sí Sí

            most elemental wound
            DOESN'T EXIST ANYMORE

Imagination loved then
    gravely respecting Death as its natural copilot
    Imagination loved then
        & that game mattered / gave birth to airs
        & if it didn't give birth to them
            the influx of earthquakes killed them without pretext
            IMAGINATION LOVED
            THEN / Yes Yes Yes Yes

---

* The name "Acuarimántima" was coined by Porfirio Barba-Jacob, the pseudonym of Colombian writer Miguel Ángel Osorio Benítez (1883–1942), and refers to a dream city in the sea.

LOU ANDREAS SALOMÉ SALUDA
A FEDERICO NIETZSCHE

La mente es 1 flor de tentáculos sin freno
pero el cuerpo es la reina
la sultana del swing
la condesa desnuda de las abejas reinas
la maja que vibra & a sí misma se da cuerda
el chapuzón de burbujas hasta el fondo
el brebaje de estrellas que se tocan
la quemadura del triángulo cuando tira sus puertas
& latidos & calambres se mojan en lo lúbrico
la Chapulín besa al Escorpión
& viceversa / & etcéteras

LOU ANDREAS SALOMÉ
GREETS FRIEDRICH NIETZSCHE

The mind is 1 flower of unbridled tentacles
but the body is queen
the sultana of swing
the queen-bee Lady Godiva
the magess that vibrates & works herself up
the bubbly dip in the depths
the brew of masturbating stars
the triangular burn when you break down her door
& heartbeats & cramps soak in lechery
Grasshopper kisses Scorpion
& vice versa / & etceteras

SAN MALCOLM EQUIS

Lamo las llagas de mi propia lepra
Esquirlas de baba
—contraesquina del azar que amaneció nublado—
golpean al corazón del ojo
—tarjeta de Tarot corpóreo—
amarrado al mástil violáceo / intralunar
Camino a Denver o a San Juan Chamula
—roto a tajadas el melón-gota de miel del superego—
El paisaje es 1 muñón de mi destino
Mi drama anterior se hunde resurgiendo
Yo & mi fantasma no sabemos *ya* si patearnos o salvarnos
¿Me llamo Malcolm o me apodo Firmin?
Estoy sudando sangre / cuajada en la ceguera de la Ilíada
((Se quema mi mar con todo & naves))
Mi muerte / a la izquierda de mis plumas
me susurra señales-piel de pólvora
que ni en trance atino a descifrar
      Escribo esto
estrujando mi seco corazón
     / Por si gotea /

SAINT MALCOLM X

I lick the wounds of my own private leprosy
Shards of drool
—cattycorner to random chance dawned overcast—
they strike the eye's heart
—the Tarot card made flesh—
bound to the purplish / intralunar mast
I walk to Denver or San Juan Chamula
—the superego's melon honey-drop in shreds—
The landscape is 1 amputation of my fate
My old drama resurfaces sinking
My ghost & I *still* don't know if we're booting or bailing ourselves out
Is my name Malcolm or do I go by Firmin*?
I'm sweating blood / clotted in the Iliad's blindness
((My sea burns ships & all))
My death / to the left of my feathers
whispers gunpowder skin-signs
that even in 1 trance I can't decipher
      I write this
wringing my dry heart
      / *In case it leaks* /

---

* A reference to Geoffrey Firmin, the protagonist of Malcolm Lowry's last complete novel, *Under the Volcano* (1947).

SAN JUAN DE LA CRUZ LE DA 1 AVENTÓN
A NEAL CASSADY / EN LA FRONTERA ENTRE
EL MITO & EL SUEÑO /

La carretera se pandea rumbo al centro de su propio incendio centrífugo
Tijuana se desvanece flotando bajo la mollera del ojo
Esquirlas de cábaret & colchón empujan la estela de duendes que
      preña la ilusión de este instante
En el radio: Jim Morrison traga esporas crecidas en la cicatriz del
      diluvio
Este puente mental va al volante
Estrellado el afuera & adentro
Verde mota la selva
El destino rodando
Todo ser & hasta en zancos escupe ovnis bordados con alas de las
      más locas luciérnagas
Es de noche / & en carretera / & volando
Los Doors con los dientes hacen realidad su voltaje
El cuerpo del alma se baña en el viaje
El centro se curva
La curva es salvaje
La carretera es Dios mismo
Cada ganglio / cada trozo
resbala: se esfuma
El pie va braceando
La mente desyerba la euforia del eco

SAINT JOHN OF THE CROSS GIVES NEAL CASSADY
1 LIFT / ON THE BORDER BETWEEN
MYTH & DREAM /

The highway warps toward the center of its own centrifugal fire
Tijuana vanishes floating under the eye's skull
Shards of cabarets & mattresses drive the file of duendes that
          impregnates this instant's illusion
On the radio: Jim Morrison swallows spores grown in the scar
          of the flood
This mental bridge grabs the wheel
Outside & inside collide
The jungle's sweet green leaf
Destiny rolling
Every being & even the 1s on stilts spit UFOs embroidered with
          the wings of lunatic fireflies
It's nighttime / & on the road / & flying
The Doors bite their voltage into reality
The spirit's body bathes in the trip
The center curves
The curve is savage
The road is God himself
Every ganglion / every slice
slips: disappears
The foot flails its arms
The mind rips euphoria's root from the echo

Mariana Larrosa aparece
reciensalidita de 1 duchazo de aguamiel & canela
las banquetas sonríen / entre la excitación & la alarma
& se oye clarito clarito cómo se desbocan
multitudes de bocinas cardiacas

Mariana Larrosa aparece
& no son sus dedos / herederos de los dedos
que a diario tan malamente nos tocan

gajos de sandía son sus ojos
frescuras envueltas en sangre
si viene de la muerte o de 1 patiovecino
si viene de dormir en la nuca de 1 árbol
o de masturbarle las antenas a 1 caracol submarino
ella nos lo va a pintar-transmitir
con manzanas con juegos

Ella que se habla de tú
con las luces fantasmas / las luces traviesas
ella que sabe de splits en do agudo
& entrechats encerrados en clósets de vidrio
ella que ahora camina & se arquea
ronronea maúlla sacude sus pliegues multiplica sus vellos
electriza zaguanes pone a volar azoteas

1 rama de dátiles
cuelga entre su boca & la mía
1 columpio de gises / listos
a colorear 1000 gargantas
administraciones de hoteles
nuestros taparrabos de espuma

Mariana Larrosa appears
fresh from 1 shower of honeywater & cinnamon
the sidewalks smile / between excitement & alarm
& clearly clearly you can hear
hordes of cardiac car horns erupting

Mariana Larrosa appears
& they're not her fingers / the heirs of her fingers
that everyday so badly touch us

watermelon wedges are her eyes
crisp fruits enveloped in blood
whether she comes from death or 1 neighboring yard
whether she comes from sleeping in the crook of 1 tree
or from masturbating 1 sea snail's antennae
she will paint it-transmit it to us
with apples with games

She who's on intimate terms
with phantom lights / mischievous lights
she who knows about splits in C sharp
& entrechats enclosed in glass closets
she who now walks & arches
purrs meows shakes her pleats multiplies her fur
electrifies hallways makes roof tiles fly

1 branch of dates
hangs between her mouth & mine
1 swing set of chalk / ready
to color 1,000 throats
hotel administrations
our loincloths of foam

ORNITORRINCA MÁS BELLA NON HABÍAMOS VISTO
los antisiquiatras le chiflan
le regalan almendras le regalan huevos de boa
a ella que es la reina de los erizos salvajes
la abejarreina de las comunas anarkas
(el naipe-túnel: la apuesta-riesgo en las brasas
quemadora de posturas & reglas que sofocan a esta especie-
        silladerruedas
                croupier paranoica de los antecomedores del póker)
¡Pagamos por ver!

Mariana Larrosa aparece / ya lo dije: lo digo: está dicho /
con este movimiento este sudor este gesto
que tiembla se emociona sonríe / cada que sé que la veo
cada que sé que la he visto & que me niego lluviosa espermática
                        atlántidamente a dejar de mirarla
& hola & quiúbole & qué jáis (entre barandales macetas techumbres
        de calor muerdeláminas)
& hola & quiúbole / & jamás ella & yo
vamos a andar por ahí borrando 1 grito
chorreando veneno desviando a otra esquina
al vagabundo chancito de matar nuestros viejos pellejos
respirar meteoritos—ocasionales incendios—
desnudarnos en sartenes de silencios calientes
citar a esta fiesta / al tiro al toque

que venga quien sepa
con su itacate de nervios su cantimplora de films o de sueños para
        pasársela rico
existan o no existan los consabidos espejos los esperados aromas
las lunasdemiel o de chicle o de calabacitas rellenas
que dicen que brotan & se vuelven presencia
llamarada colchón conversación importante
apenas cruzas de 1 brinco apenas te acercas gateando
a la espinosa frontera cercada de flechas letreros

WE'VE NEVER SEEN SUCH PRETTY PLATYPUSSY
the antipsychiatrists catcall
regale her with almonds with boa eggs
she who is queen of the wild hedgehogs
the queen bee of anarkist communes
(playingcard-tunnel: the wager in hot coals
burner of postures & rules that suffocate this wheelchair-species
                              paranoid breakfast table poker croupier)
        We pay to watch!

Mariana Larrosa appears / I said it already: I say it: it's said /
with this movement this sweat this gesture
that trembles gets excited smiles / for all I know I see her
for all I know I have seen her & deny myself rainy spermatic
                              atlantically when I cease to look at her
& hey & what's up & what's goin' on (between handrails flower pots
        heated rooftops bite-plates)
& hey & what's up / & she & I will never again
walk around there erasing 1 scream
dripping venom crossing the street to avoid
the little vagabond chance to kill our old hides
breathe meteorites—sometimes fires—
get naked in pans of hot silence
meet up at this party / straight off on the spot

let whoever comes come
with their lunchbag of nerves their canteen of films or dreams
        of living the good life
whether or not they exist the proverbial mirrors the expected aromas
the honey or chewing gum moons or moons of stuffed squash
that say they bloom & become presence
distress signal cushion important conversation
you barely leap in 1 bound you barely reach crawling
the spiked border surrounded with arrows signs

que indican los más cercanos hoteles para después de morir

Mariana Larrosa aparece
baterista de su propio baile
cuerda-yerbacrecida de su único e inimitable swing

              pointing to the closest postmortem hotels

Mariana Larrosa appears
drummer of her own dance
herb-grown cord of her single & inimitable swing

AULLIDO DE CISNE

Atorado en los pasillos del Hotel Esfinge
El hombre es 1 ser temporal
& contingente / lanzado entre 2 nadas
Amarrado a su propia percepción
Floreado de azar entre luna & nalga
Cosido al garfio de su espíritu
& goteando cuerpo a lo largo & a lo ancho
de los infinitos campos de concentración
   Cenit & Nadir
   : tal es su signo :
 / la horca labrada en su molleja /
El gesto calcinado vomita aún fulgor
El hombre es 1 rey moral aunque astringente
Mariposa de Extranja
Murciélago que rompe el saco
que transporta su asfixiada concepción

Nació como de la gota el cielo
& como del hueso el axial dolor
Abismo de herradura entre montañas
Constelación-festín de hormigas rojas
Beso sin alas donde muere el río
El hombre es 1 ser celestial amuñonado
Sintaxis estrellada
Albedrío del corazón
/ que a tamtams se desboca & se detiene
subrayándole los párpados al vértigo
ahogando en semen al fantasma de toda explicación /

Ahora & siempre

El camino está hecho

SWAN'S HOWL

Trapped in the corridors of the Hotel Sphinx
Man is 1 temporal & contingent
being / thrust between 2 nothings
Bound to his own perception
Flowering at random between moon & buttocks
Sewn to the hook of his spirit
& leaking body from all sides
of the infinite concentration camps
                    Zenith & Nadir
                    : such is his sign :
    / the gallows stamped in his entrails /
The charred visage still vomits splendor
Man is 1 moral if astringent king
1 butterfly of the Outside
1 bat that bursts the sac
carrying its strangled conception

Heaven was born as if from gout
& axial pain as if from bone
1 hairpin cleft between mountains
1 banquet constellation of red ants
1 wingless kiss where the river ends
Man is 1 sawed-off celestial being
Syntax decked in stars
The heart's will
/ that runs wild & stops short to the beat of the drum
underlining vertigo's eyelids
drowning the ghost of all explanations in semen /

Now & forever

The way is made

: Convulsiónate :
Las leyes del Espacio se rematan
suicidado el tiempo que llagaba el destino del timón
 Caló es vivir & acalambrarse es tocho
La luz se mete la verga a sí misma
bajo el puente ahíto del electroshock
La muerte es el fuego que revive
al cochambre en bruto de la cacerola
La muerte no es muerte
Su eterna cicatriz florea
Como voz de parto
O como voz / sencillamente /
Como flor de voz
Aquí el *Tú* es *Yo*
Cogidos de ella la ratonera & el ratón
Hace 1 ratón *** farfulló el Génesis
La cantina de su buche goteaba lagartijas
bragueta abajo de su irreal banqueta
/ Las hipótesis se demuestran paladeándolas /
André Breton come caca
Se alimenta el *ser* del *no ser*
El pulpo & la culebra cogen estallando
            —Cara al Caos—
La mitología es real & chifla ahorita
1 ecuación la dejó plantada

De los días terrenales al apando
1 mandrágora transforma su veneno en aroma de mujer
        :: *deípara flagrante* ::
La voluntad estelar alburea
Te sientas a masticarle el eco   su película de siglos
/ filmada & sudada dentro del congal *El don de la risa* /

Ahora sí es marzo
—alto mes de la magia—

: Convulse yourself :
The laws of Space are finished
the time that flayed the rudder's fate committed suicide
Living bites & cramping up is lame
The light sticks its dick in itself
under the glutted electroshock bridge
Death is the fire that resurrects
the frying pan's raw scum
Death is not death
Its eternal scar flowers
Like the voice of childbirth
Or like the voice / simply /
Like the flower of voice
Here the *You* is *I*
It's been chicken-hawks & chickens
Since the first *** cock crowed Genesis
The flask in its maw dripped lizards
its unreal sidewalk's fly was down
/ Hypotheses are proved by tasting them /
André Breton eats shit
Being feeds on *non-being*
The octopus & the snake screw exploding
　　　　—Facing Chaos—
Mythology is real & whistles at the moment
1 equation leaves it in the lurch

From earthly days to the prison cell
1 mandrake turns its venom to the scent of 1 woman
　　　:: godbirth in flagrante ::
Puns the stellar will
You sit down to chew the echo　its film of centuries
/ sweated & shot in 1 brothel called *The Gift of Laughter* /

Now it really is March
—high month of magic—

89

Eyacula la liebre en 1 libre
que chilla en las curvas / ardiendo de uñas a halo

¡Se encueró la esencia!
vocea el paletero

Mientras que 2 lóbulos flechan sus flujos
en el cráter mismo en que nace 1 esquina

Hoy / ayer & siempre

En el íris íntimo de todas las bestias
Que lamen a ciencia & conciencia el último tumor del crepúsculo

Mato lo que digo
:: Aullido de Cisne ::

The rabbit ejaculates in 1 taxi
that whines around curves / burning from fingernails to halo

They stripped essence bare!
cries the ice cream man

While 2 lobes shoot their juices
in the very crater where 1 corner is born

Now / yesterday & forever

In the intimate iris of all beasts
That lick the final tumor of twilight from consciousness & science

    I kill what I speak
    :: Swan's howl ::

SÁCALE LA FLAMA AL DIABLO

Para el Poncho Soriano

1 clochard mexicano llamado Gautier
Chinche ambulante
Lo más lejos del ruido lechoso de esta vaga ciudad
Incrustada en su coño
Como mosca ladeándose en la orilla de 1 sope
Su botella / dormida & soñándose
1 frío de la gran puta
Toda ilusión destrozada
Pero él sueña & lo hace deveras
Vuela entre grietas
Recorre el olvidado olor de mágicos bosques
Es mexicano & su apodo: franchute revuelto en ajenjo
Con la letra que arranca su nombre
nos enseñaron de chavos a gargarear borborigmos
Hoy / la luz Lucifer de los otros
se le escama
se hunde
glugluteante se resbala & se pela
Él se rasca rebotando en sí mismo
No hay banca de parque
ni ojos de hada
que le den albergue o sustento
Es 1 chingón de los buenos
Muerto sí / Pero en vida /
En el trompo jugoso sangrante de esta vida risueña
Así como no hay dientes sin boca
Ni gatos chillones sin ratas
Ni musgo sin verde
Ni sol que de pendejo no se caiga a lamer el aroma de cualquier
      torva azotea

STEAL FIRE FROM THE DEVIL

For Poncho Soriano

1 Mexican tramp called Gautier
1 walking bedbug
Farthest from the milky noise of this vague city
Embedded in its cunt
Like 1 fly inclined on the rim of 1 *sope*
His bottle / asleep & dreaming
1 motherfucker of 1 chill
Every illusion destroyed
But he dreams & makes it real
Flies between cracks
Relives the forgotten scent of magic forests
He's Mexican & his nickname: frenchie scrambled in absinthe
With the letter that begins his name
we were taught as kids to gargle hunger pangs
Now / the Lucifer light of the others
gets under his skin
he collapses
gobbling away he slips & peels out
He gets scratched up bouncing off himself
There's no park bench
no fairy eyes
to give him room or board
He's 1 badass of 1 good guy
Dead yes / But in life /
In the juicy bleeding spin of this smiling life
Just as there are no teeth without 1 mouth
No screeching cats without 1 mouse
No moss without the color green
& no idiot sun that won't descend to lap the scent of any
 sinister rooftop

CALLEJÓN SIN SALIDA

Callejón sin salida / ayúdanos
a ensanchar nuestros sentidos
Tú tan ninguneado
cueva / desierto / metrópoli filosa
árida ranchería / témpano cortante
puente dilatado por 1 gas
que de repente pulveriza
los inencontrables tréboles de 4 hojas
que oxigenan alimentan prestan sus alas
a tus pulmones heridos / a las pezuñas de canguro
                                con que avanzan tus orillas
Callejón sin salida
tablita pirata
salto de tigre
transpiración entre la niebla
LSD escurridizo
rostro en el que vemos beber
chupar su fuerza
a las especies más nómadas
de nuestros árboles de fuego
Callejón sin salida
voz de los inquietos
canción de los difíciles
biombo de cerezos
que escogen para sus muecas los travestis
Inyección de ¡bastas!
papiro con signos
al que sólo los imbéciles
son capaces de no entregar su vista
Cuna de motines
incubadora de orgasmos
hamaca carnívora

DEAD END STREET

Dead end street / help us
to enlarge our senses
You that everyone ignores
cavern / desert / cutthroat metropolis
desert shantytown / jagged iceberg
bridge extended by 1 gas
that suddenly pulverizes
the unobtainable 4 leaf clovers
that oxygenate nourish lend wings
to your wounded lungs / to the kangaroo hooves
                  of your advancing banks
Dead end street
pirate's plank
tiger's pounce
sweat in the fog
slippery LSD
face in which we see the strength
of the most nomadic species
of our flame trees
being sucked & drunk
Dead end street
voice of the restless
song of the difficult
cherry blossom screen
transvestites choose to make their faces
Injections of *Enough!*
papyrus with signs
from which only imbeciles
can avert their eyes
Cradle of mutinies
incubator of orgasms
carnivorous hammock

en la que medito los jugos de jazz
con los que saldré más fresco
más brillante / de mis próximos incendios
Aparentemente tú has decidido darnos la espalda
acordonarnos los músculos del cuello
triturarnos los fusibles
jugar con nosotros al festín de los fantasmas
Pero lo cierto en este crucigrama
de barricadas temblonas
camas destendidas
citas inciertas
con lo desconocido intrauterino
Pero lo cierto en este crucigrama
es que la lengua del poeta te visita
el sudor del guerrillero penetra en ti / hasta los ojos
los fetos electrizados del deseo aún insatisfecho
bailan con tus vértebras
forjan sus flautines
prenden sus inciensos en tu pelvis
Mientras tú les sonríes les conversas
les regalas gasolina / soma vibrátil
dentaduras trepadoras que arrancas de ti mismo
& ya puedes considerarte
socio : cómplice : infrarrealista hermanito nuestro
Crucemos cojos / desgreñados / o cantando
los gises polvorientos de esta raya
Callejón sin salida
autostop que me doy a mí mismo
Tu muslo izquierdo : enfermedad
tu muslo derecho : medicina
A la hora en que cierran sus taquillas
los centros nocturnos & los circos
En el momento en que se desmaya la venta de aspirinas consoladores
        hexámetros famosos
es que tú apareces

where I contemplate the juices of jazz
with which I'll emerge fresher
more brilliant / from my next fires
Apparently you've decided to turn your back on us
to cordon off the muscles of our necks
crush our fuses
act out the feast of the dead with us
But what's certain in this crossword puzzle
of trembling barricades
unmade beds
dubious meetings
with the intrauterine unknown
But what's certain in this crossword puzzle
is that the poet's tongue visits you
the guerrilla's sweat penetrates / up to your eyes
the electrified fetuses of unsatisfied desire
dance in your vertebrae
forge their piccolos
light their incense in your pelvis
While you smile at them chat with them
give them gasoline / resonant soma
creeping teeth yanked from your own mouth
& now you can consider yourself
our partner : accomplice : our infrarealist little brother
Let's limp across / disheveled / or singing /
this line of crumbling chalk
Dead end street
free ride I hitch with myself
Your left thigh : sickness
your right thigh : medicine
When the nightclubs & circuses
close their ticket booths
At the moment the sale of aspirin dildos famous hexameters passes
        out
that's when you appear

en vías de tatuarnos bajo la piel
el rasguño primero de nuestro más obsesivo autorretrato
& ya hasta te silbamos entre sueños
& preferimos salir contigo & con cero pasaportes
a estas calles / bulevares de moho
pasadizos lechosos / vías directas a la hemorragia ámbar
Callejón sin salida
dínos con 1 ojo
rehileteando 1 pestaña
hacia dónde disparar
suave / febrilmente
nuestra última mirada-picahielo
nuestros últimos cartuchos
remolinos de clara vida & fresco semen
Para la normalidad estamos muertos
para la logística militar no existimos
para las gélidas aguas del cálculo bursátil
nuestras escamas / nuestras hélices son encías fantasmagóricas
coágulos irresistibles de 1 resplandor
que nos pretenden negar a escopetazos
Pero tú bien sabes
que muy muy dentro de ti
acariciamos probamos tu bocado
rajamos para siempre
las alfombras sin luz propia del horóscopo
Callejón sin salida
Callejón de muervida
socio : cómplice : infrarrealista hermanito nuestro

about to tattoo under our skin
the first scratch of our most obsessive self-portrait
& now we even whistle to you in dreams
& prefer to go out with you & with zero passports
on these streets / boulevards of mold
milky corridors / fast lanes to the amber hemorrhage
Dead end street
tell us with 1 eye
darting 1 single lash
where to shoot
softly / feverishly
our final icepick gaze
our final cartridges
whirlwinds of clear life & fresh semen
We're dead to normality
according to military logistics we don't exist
according to the frigid waters of market calculation
our fish scales / our propellers are ghostly toothless gums
irresistible clots of 1 radiance
they attempt to deny us at gunpoint
But you know well
that deep down inside you
we caress we taste every morsel you eat
we slash once and for all
the planets' light-reflecting carpets
Dead end street
street of the living dead
partner : accomplice : our infrarealist little brother

ECCE HOMO

Caído de la nube menos proclive al estallido
Sin embargo / rebelde a ese amargo tronco
Gota a gota rana & musgo
expiación de pedruzco sin cascada
Desangro como a toro por los cuernos
el muñón resbaloso al que se aferra mi albedrío
Soy abeja africana que supera toda trampa
Dios exacto se hinca a mamarle la verga a Dios demente
Caín se le regala a Abel transformado en ajolote
         de mirra & cempazúchitl
No habrá otro espejo más cercano a las heridas de mi lengua
Soy aquél que llora
que coge lo poco que se encuentra
La caries que se chupa la mujer por no morderme
El arca de la Alianza confundida
El ala gambusina
La inabsorbible sangre
Los kilos de cerilla acumulada
tras la barda de vidrio de mi oreja anestesiada
Soy el último patio del último manicomio no dopado
Ni tengo sexo / Ni respeto a nadie
Gocé vivir
Beso a mi muerte
La empuño
la columpio
la salpico
la derrocho
No hay larva a quien no contagie de mi virus
Al miércoles de ceniza lo convierto en jueves
Porque son santos todos los balazos
Desde el primero al último

ECCE HOMO

Fallen from the cloud least likely to explode
Nevertheless / in revolt against this bitter trunk
Drop by drop frog & moss
torrentless atonement of rough stone
I drain the blood like 1 bull by the horns
of the slimy stump my will clings to
I'm the African bee that outsmarts every trap
The exact God kneels to blow the deranged God's cock
Cain gives himself to Abel transformed as 1 salamander of
          marigold & myrrh
There shall be no mirror closer to the wounds of my tongue
I'm the 1 that cries
that grabs the little he finds
The cavity the woman sucks in order not to bite me
The confused Arc of the Covenant
The snipe's wing
The unabsorbable blood
The kilos of wax accumulated
behind the glass fence of my anesthetized solar ear
I'm the last courtyard of the last undrugged asylum
I have no sex / I respect nobody
I enjoyed being alive
I kiss my death
I grasp it
I swing it
I splash it
I squander it
There's no larva that hasn't caught my virus
I turn Ash Wednesday into Thursday
Because all bullet wounds are sacred
From the first to the last

VAS A MORIR COMO 1 GANGLIO DE LUZ QUE SE HA VUELTO LOCO VAS A MORIR / ENTRE SILENCIOS COJOS

Para Sid Vicious & Elvis Costello

Decir amor / muerte / hambre / sexo/ ratas / de otro modo: para ser comprendido de otro modo /
José Revueltas /
cárcel preventiva de la ciudad de México / octubre de 1969

Elvis canta
  Elvis se quema
    se desgarra la garganta

Ha andado con suerte
el rock de la cárcel / no ha podido fundirlo

Sólo los espejismos moros se enamoran

La garganta se anuda
  & no llega a desanudarse

pero la luz que hay en mí
  se niega a extinguirse

No hay aerolito
al que no le pida STOP
no hay carretera
a la que no le arrebate 1 beso

Toco el día / en la calle
trepando postes de luz
ordeñando postes de luz
patinando vértebra a vértebra
esta ciudad de entrañas oscuras

YOU'LL DIE LIKE 1 GANGLION OF LIGHT GONE MAD
YOU'LL DIE / BETWEEN CRIPPLED SILENCES

For Sid Vicious & Elvis Costello

*To say love / death / hunger / sex / rats / in
another way: to be understood in another way /
José Revueltas /
Mexico City detention center / October 1969*

Elvis sings
  Elvis burns
    he tears his throat

He's been lucky
the jailhouse rock / hasn't melted him

Only fool illusions fall in love

The throat's tied in knots
  it can't untangle

but the light that's inside me
  won't be extinguished

There's no meteorite
I wouldn't hitch 1 ride on
no highway
I wouldn't steal 1 kiss from

I touch day / in the street
scaling lamp posts
milking lamp posts
skating through this city of dark bowels
vertebra by vertebra

la selva-apocalipsis de 1980 marchita mi paso

Alegría escupe zanjas
  Esperanza pare círculos
    Audacia se ahuma a sí misma
      Paradoja no sabe a qué otra circuncisión inciensar
hasta que *Saltomortal*
la despierta salpicándole cascadas
ríos de cul-de-sacs / callejones sin salida que son agua
saliva alfilereada de su propio mar de angustia
Vas a morir como 1 ganglio de luz
        que se ha vuelto loco
Vas a morir / entre silencios cojos

the 1980 jungle-apocalypse withers my stride

Joy spits up ditches
  Hope gives birth to circles
    Daring smokes itself out
      Paradox doesn't know what other circumcision to burn
        for incense
until *Deathplunge*
spatters it with waterfalls to wake it up
cul-de-sac rivers / dead end streets that are water
slivers of saliva from its own sea of anguish
You'll die like 1 ganglion of light
      gone mad
You'll die / between crippled silences

DICTADO EN 1 SUEÑO

& sin embargo
en el corazón de la rosa de 100 pétalos
en el puente que divide al amor / de turbias furias
en el ojo de la gruta iluminada
en el fondo del río que nos aclara
el misterio sigue ahí
filoagudo / fisiolúdico
como 1 lluvia prendida
que no respeta ciudad
madriguera / rapto mental / nobleza de aguas
Aletazos de ciego tras la vara de ámbar
Así de cabrón / *valedor*

DICTATED IN 1 DREAM

& nevertheless
in the heart of the 100-petaled rose
on the bridge dividing love / from turbid furies
in the eye of the illuminated cave
at the bottom of the purifying river
the mystery holds its ground
razortoothed / physioludic
like 1 burning rain
that respects no city
rabbit hole / mental rapture / aristocracy of waters
Flappings in the dark beyond the amber rod
That kind of badass / *homeboy*

LA REALIDAD MANCHA

Cercados entre *sinchos* & *netas*
La ronda de borrachos abraza el lote baldío de sus sombras
/ 1 recuerda el primer dadá de su primera hija
Otro la noche en que su ex musa levitaba
Aquél tararea destello a destello la magia flameada de 1 rocola
        cercana /
Estrellita marinera agita sus aguas
Dibuja en silencio el cuerpo rotundo de ese momento luminoso
Eones que rompen / vértebra a vértebra /
la fiebre esculpida de 1 invisible carcaj
Arqueros del cielo
que cubre la piel labradita de esta loca tierra
Trepa la espuma : equilibrista :
La mente ordeña al vago cuerpo
que alberga su aire / preñado en pleno vuelo
¡Rueda 1 triste gota de sol!
1 vidrito de la divinidad rasga de sopetón a las gargantas
Me dan ganas de orinar 1 arcoiris
de besarle la panocha a la necesidad
& pararme de cabeza / ¡de regalo!
Juez & parte de esta bocanada de parranda cósmica
lloro como Marcel Duchamp frente al *Gran Vidrio*
& ya no sé si soy la pedrada o soy el brazo
la última horca / el amanecer del soy
Está suspendida la gravedad como otra mosca más en flor de loto
No hemos salido aún de los callejones de Verona
El invento de Romeo condena a la insania a William Shakespeare
& me atrevo a decir que la tal Julieta
le mama la verga a más de 3 políticos priistas
En el garage del Hotel Gólgota
—camello que eructa en el ojo de 1 aguja—
& no precisamente en los ensayos de 1 comedia musical

REALITY STAINS

Surrounded by *yeps* & *no shits*
The circle of drunks hugs the vacant lot of their shadows
/ 1 remembers his first daughter's first dada
Another the night his ex-muse levitated
1 guy hums the flaming magic of 1 nearby jukebox in flashes /
1 starfish stirs its waters
Silently draws the rounded body of this luminous moment
Eons that break / vertebra by vertebra /
the sculpted fever of 1 invisible quiver
Archers of the sky
that covers the chiseled skin of this crazy earth
The foam climbs : funambulist :
The mind milks the lazy body
that houses its air / pregnant in full flight
1 sad sundrop rolls down!
1 shard of divinity suddenly slashes their throats
It makes me want to piss 1 rainbow
to lick necessity's pussy
& stand on my head / for free!
Judge and jury of this cosmic binge
I cry like Marcel Duchamp in front of the *Large Glass*
& don't know anymore if I'm the stone or the arm that hurls it
the last ditch / dawn of the I am
Gravity is suspended like 1 more fly in the lotus flower
We haven't even left the alleys of Verona
The invention of Romeo condemns William Shakespeare to madness
& I dare say that girl Juliet
sucks the dicks of more than 3 PRIist politicians
In the garage of the Hotel Golgotha
—1 camel belching in the eye of 1 needle—
& not exactly in rehearsals for 1 musical comedy

DESESPEJO

A la memoria de Beltrán Morales
Con música de fondo de Javier Solís

Mural de alcohólicos el día
Explosión: la noche eterna
El viento encarnado en hueso florido de mujer
En vagancia de niños tras los sueños del flautista
Lo demás es muerte en vida
Convivencia de ratas & alacranes
/ *en tiempos & espacios diferentes* /
Pero atados al tufo que traza el arcoiris de 1 a otro horno crematorio
Donde de seguro 2 locos reposan dándose 1 son
La bugambilia le rasca la ingle al polvo de la cruz
El sol es la multiplicación continua
El canto de la luz
El *tour de force* de lo creado
Que se mueve / sin embargo /
en el mundo—tordo gratis—como mariposa azul
Picasso se muerde la cola
—embarrado de follaje humano—
Silba el fantasma del globero
Suelta su hilo la semilla
La persigue ((entre navajas))
la certeza estratosférica del eco
La Belleza es nuestra Guernica espiritual
El retrato de Galatea empinándose en 1 pozo
/ culo fresco: *porno movie* de candor no natural /
Gordos & flacos ruedan por la herida abierta
El náufrago continúa en el agua / filmándose a sí mismo /
Tiempo de besar al destino
        ¡Como sea!
Está escrito en mi cuerpo encenizado
En la brama muda de otros cuerpos

DISMIRROR

To the memory of Beltrán Morales
With background music by Javier Solís

The day 1 mural of drunks
Explosion: eternal night
Wind made flesh in woman's flowering bone
Wandering like children through the piper's dreams
The rest is living death
Marriage of rats & scorpions
/ *in different times & spaces* /
But tied to the stench the rainbow traces from 1 crematorium to the next
Where no doubt 2 madmen recline getting high
Bougainvillea scratches 1 crotch with the dust of the cross
The sun is perpetual multiplication
The song of light
The *tour de force* of the created
That moves / nevertheless /
through the world—free songbird—like 1 blue butterfly
Picasso bites his tail
—caked with human foliage—
The balloon man's specter hisses
The seed opens its eye
The echo's stratospheric truth
pursues it ((at knifepoint))
Beauty is our spiritual Guernica
The portrait of Galatea getting in up in 1 well
/ fresh ass: unnaturally honest porn flick /
Laurels & Hardys tumble through the open wound
The castaway stays in the water / filming himself /
Time to kiss fate
     So be it!
Is written on my charred body
In the mute bellow of other bodies

que se abisman en el vientre aparente de sus yos
Todos somos Marías Sabinas conversando con los ángeles
Pero lo olvidamos / abrumados por la pena de no reconocernos
:: Fracciones de segundo / lunas imantadas /
mordeduras de éter que masturban al sol ::

that bury themselves in the visible womb of the I
We're all María Sabinas talking with the angels
But we forget / overwhelmed by the pain of not knowing ourselves
:: Fractions of 1 second / magnetized moons /
ether bites that masturbate the sun ::

CANCIÓN IMPLACABLE

Me cago en Dios
& en todos sus muertos
Me cago en la hostia
& en el coñito de la virgen
Me cago en los muertos
del Dios de Dios
en la soberbia de Federico Nietzche
en el cuerpo tembloroso de mi alma
& en las ortigas al aire del ateo
en la muerte prematura de los justos
en la fugacidad del coito & sus centellas
En el verbo animal
En la imaginación-rizoma
En los textos del saber tan destetado
En la raja de los mundos
Yo me cago
Concentrado en el incendio de mis poros
en este alcohol-maleza que me cimbra
en el ojo infinito de mis huellas
en el furor salvaje del desmadre
en la imposible muerte & sus ofrendas
En el barro de áspid que calienta
en las rocas de la amada
en la levitación de mi calaca
en el cojo corazón de lo innombrable
En el aleph acuoso de mis llagas
en la vítrea desazón de mi asesino
en la mano del placer
en la droga anidada en sus colmillos
En el ogro filantrópico & su esposa
en la tumba del azar tan manoseada
en el germen de la lírica / que es caca

RELENTLESS SONG

I shit on God
& all his dead
I shit on the sacrament
& on the virgin's little cunt
I shit on the dead
of the God of God
on the arrogance of Friedrich Nietzsche
on my soul's trembling flesh
& on the airborne thorns of the atheist
on the premature death of the just
on the transience of sex & its sparks
On the animal word
On the imagination-rhizome
On the desiccated teats of learning
On the cleft of worlds
I shit
Focused on the fire of my pores
on this alcohol-sickness that shakes me
on the infinite eye of my footprints
on the bacchanal's savage fury
on impossible death & its offerings
On the mud of the asp warming itself
on the rocks of the beloved
on my skull's levitation
on the crippled heart of the unnamable
On the aqueous aleph of my wounds
on my killer's vitreous malaise
on the hand of pleasure
on the drug nestled in its fangs
On the philanthropic ogre & his wife
on the hackneyed tomb of chance
on the germ of the lyric / which is caca

En la boñiga aérea
en las lagañas topas
en el cráneo todo esplendor de Charleville
En las ratas que aún huyen del Mar Ebrio
en lo blando
en lo fofo
& en lo inerme
En el eructo de éter de los sapos
en las sangres hirvientes
en las sombras
en el rosa gargajo de las albas
en el vidrio insensato que he escogido como calle
en las barrancas de Venus tumefacta
En el platón del festín
en las bacinicas de la tregua
en el hongo podrido & su tridente
En el genealógico tumor de la US Army
en el extenso linaje de la mierda
Abismo & resplandor / azar & viento
Vena abierta de cocxis a clavícula
Regazo de embriaguez
Llama de arpas embozadas
En las ingles sin axilas de Dios-inventamuertos
en el suave & múltiple rumor que hacen 2 lágrimas
: en el mar : en sus desiertos :
& en mí mismo

On aerial horseshit
on gopher eye-crust
on Charleville's resplendent cranium
On the rats still fleeing the Drunken Sea
on tenderness
on flabbiness
& on defenselessness
On toads' etheric belches
on boiling blood
on shadows
on the dawn's rosy phlegm-ball
on the insensible mirror I've picked for a street
on the canyons of tumescent Venus
On the banquet platter
on the bedpans of truce
on the rotten mushroom & its trident
On the genealogical tumor of the US Army
on the long lineage of crap
Abyss & radiance / chance & wind
Open vein from coccyx to clavicle
Lap of inebriation
Flame of muffled harps
On the crotchless groins of death-creating God
on the soft & varied hum 2 teardrops make
: on the sea : on its deserts :
& on myself

ÚNICA SANGRE

Para Rebeca López

Naciste del semen de Gerard de Nerval
Exactamente a las plantas de su horca
De sus ojos radiantes / destrozados
De la entraña de su videncia inmaculada
De su poderosa mente extraterrena
De su charrasqueado & singular destino
Brotaste / buscándome
Enfrentando los océanos imposibles
Librando el albedrío de las tormentas
/ *Como fuera* /
Con tal de llegar a besar todas mis llagas
A los pies alados de esa misma horca
De la que también soy hijo

SINGLE BLOOD

For Rebeca López

You were born from the sperm of Gérard de Nerval
Right at the base of his scaffold
From his radiant / shattered eyes
From the entrails of his immaculate clairvoyance
From his strong extraterrestrial mind
From his scarred / singular fate
You blossomed / in search of me
Confronting impossible oceans
Liberating the will of storms
/ *By any means* /
Just to be able to kiss all my sores
At the winged feet of that same scaffold
From which I too was born

MIENTRAS ESCUCHAMOS ABRAZADOS *LOVE HER MADLY* DEL GRUPO THE DOORS

Quiero a mi hija / como se quiere a 1 río de carne concretita
      personal e inimitable
pájara gozosa de 6 meses
sirenita lactante
risa sentida a 5 filos de sol o baño en tina
Sus cagadas son oro
sus meadas 1 néctar
Pinche Zirita loca / canto
al hacerle 1 rehilete o estrellarnos como avión
Tiene 1 muñeca mulata
tiene un garabato punk
le vacila hasta el lodo del mundo
lo patea con sus ojos extremos
Cachorrita tacubayense
cactus secreto de México
Todavía no conoce el mar / el vaivén sexual
el corazón desatado de las calles-peyote
El día que suba a 1 tren
a 1 naranja de nieve
que brinque de 1 salto de Jalapa a Moscú
que le diga a la luna / cháchara
que le diga a la luna / gorda
que platique con Joan Miró
& rompa 1 cassette de los Beatles
Ya la estoy oyendo gritarles / ¡chafas!
a los ¾ del mundo
Los opaca con sus pestañas
los ofende con su ombliguito
Toda ella 1 sonaja
No se parece a nadie
la muerte le sabe el ansia
la vida se lo subraya

WHILE LISTENING IN EACH OTHER'S ARMS
TO THE DOORS' *LOVE HER MADLY*

I love my daughter / like 1 loves 1 river of absolutely concrete
      intimate & inimitable flesh
Joyful 6-month bird-girl
nursing little mermaid
laughter felt in 5 blades of sunlight or 1 bathtub
Her poop is gold
her pee is nectar
Crazy damned Zirita / I sing
making her 1 pinwheel or crashing us like 1 airplane
She has 1 mulatto dolly
She vibrates like punk graffiti
swings toward the mud of the world
kicks it with her extreme eyes
Tacubayense puppy
Mexico's secret cactus
She still doesn't know the sea / the rocking of sex
the unbound heart of peyote-streets
The day she mounts 1 train
or 1 orange of snow
that leaps from Jalapa to Moscow in 1 single bound
let her call the moon / gossip
let her call the moon / fatty
let her flirt with Joan Miró
& break 1 Beatles cassette
I already hear her shouting / phonies!
at ¾ of the world
Her eyelashes overshadow them
Her little bellybutton offends them
All of her is 1 rattle
She's unlike anyone else
death tastes her yearning
life underlines it

Nació 1 miércoles de ceniza
1 día de amplias cervezas
Llegó con su barquito pirata
como a 1 boca 1 ostión

She was born 1 Ash Wednesday
1 day of many beers
She arrived in her little pirate boat
like 1 oyster to 1 mouth

ESCUDO DE CRIN : BRAZOS DE CRISTAL

A la memoria de Juan Nicolás Arturo Rimbaud

¡Con cuántos pelones o greñudos no te han confundido!
A las orillas de tus propios vértices
Desafiando la visión erecta de tu sombra
/ Saliva bailando entre los dientes /

Todos quisimos ser ese niño
que enlodaba de misterio a los escribas

Impulso insensato e infinito hacia los esplendores invisibles
¡Las voces reconstituídas; el despertar fraterno de todas las
*   energías corales & orquestales*
& sus aplicaciones instantáneas; la ocasión, única, de liberar
*   nuestros sentidos!*

Después del Diluvio no has vuelto
Juan Nicolás Arturo

Tu homosexualismo era panteista & al revés
El solo nombre de Verlaine significa absolutamente todo esto
Tu definitivo amor al cosmos
:: Sus milagros / sus desastres
su fortuna / su peligro ::
Pero el cuerpo es 1 tesoro que prodigar
& tú lo hiciste
Culeaste con los soles de la Psyche
Penetraste a la Diosa misma en su capullo
Cabrón tan esperma / tan óvulo
            Única flor hermafrodita
            Te beso & te extraño
            Carnal de mi tormenta
            mi embriaguez & mis heridas

HORSEHAIR SHIELD : GLASS ARMS

To the memory of Jean Nicolas Arthur Rimbaud

What gangbanger or longhair haven't they pegged you for!
On the shores of your own vertices
Defying the rock-hard vision of your shadow
/ Spit dancing between your teeth /

We all wanted to be that boy
who smeared the scribes with mystery

Insensate & infinite impulsion toward invisible splendors
Reconstituted voices; the brotherly awakening of all energies
        choral & orchestral
& their instant application; the occasion, the only 1, to liberate
        our senses!

After the Flood you didn't come back
Jean Nicolas Arthur

Your homosexuality was pantheist & vice versa
The mere name of Verlaine signifies all this
Your ultimate love of the cosmos
:: Its miracles / its disasters
its fortune / its danger ::
But the body is 1 treasure to squander
& you did it
You buggered Psyche's suns
You penetrated the cunt of the Goddess herself
1 sonofabitch so spermatic / so ovular
        Singular hermaphroditic flower
        I kiss you & I miss you
        Blood brother of my storm
        my drunkenness my wounds

SIN EMBARGO SOBREVUELO
COMO 1 DINASTÍA DE SOLES

A la memoria de Alejandra Pizarnik

¿A dónde me conduce esta escritura?
/ rosa de aspavientos: espantapájaros /
¿A qué falo de sol remojado en espuma de alabanzas?
Si no me suicido hoy / ya me suicidaré mañana
Querido amigo:
La risa en la agonía es cascada flamígera
Vivir & llagarse
llegarse / bucearse
romper el hechizo
cantar / sin piedad /
No sé
((piedra bicorne))
((vihuela rapaz))
Ni el camino de la lengua
ni las leguas a Bagdad
Odio esta *Caricatura Divina*
& en medio esta verga oscura
que llora alucinada
rompiendo todo vergel
¿La noche por siempre noche?
Es de imbécil & poeta preguntar
Comenzar por el final la quemadura
Acercarse a la ardidera
/ como ángel en su óvulo /
El infierno—llama a llama—es musical
La cola del dragón es su granalla
¿Esquirlas de la mente?
¿Alebrijes?
Estos días terrenales
han sido mi haikú / mi harakiri
¿Quién chingaos seré yo?

I FLY OVERHEAD NONETHELESS
LIKE 1 DYNASTY OF SUNS

To the memory of Alejandra Pizarnik

Where does this writing lead me?
/ wildly gesticulating rose: scarecrow /
To what solar phallus drenched in the foam of praise?
If I don't kill myself today / I'll kill myself tomorrow
Dear friend:
Laughter in agony is 1 flaming waterfall
To live & to fester
to arrive / to dive under
to break the spell
to sing / without piety /
I don't know
((double-edged stone))
((ravening lyre))
Neither the road of language
nor the leagues to Baghdad
I hate this *Divine Caricature*
& this dark prick in the middle
weeping with astonishment
destroying every orchard
Is the night forever night?
It is for the fool & the poet to ask
To begin at the end of the burn
To approach the breaking point
/ like 1 angel in ovum /
The inferno—its every flame—is musical
Its shrapnel is dragon's tail
Shards of the mind?
Tchotchkes?
These days on earth
have been my haiku / my hara-kiri
Who the fuck am I going to be?

A LA MANERA DE OMAR KHAYAM

Para Norman Sverdlin

Desde mi risco más álgido
Aura de mi intemperie
Jardín de mi desquebrajadura
Desfiladero de azules casi en veta
　/ Yoyamín entero /
Deposito esta perla
En la Gruta de Venus
((*Mi Roshanikrá amada*))
Sin la que yo no sería
　　Ni esperma
　　Ni utopía
　　Ni Nada

IN THE STYLE OF OMAR KHAYAM

For Norman Sverdlin

From the peak of my cliff
My weatherbeaten aura
Garden of my rupture
Ravine of near inveterate blues
   / Solid Yoyamín /
I deposit this pearl
In the Grotto of Venus
((*My precious Rosh Hanikra*))
Without which I'd be
      Neither sperm
      Nor utopia
      Nor anything

¿ESTO SE DICE O SE BERREA?

Odio la carroña
Adoro la vida
Conmigo se volvió loca la anatomía
Soy todo corazón

DO YOU SAY THIS OR SHRIEK IT?

I hate carrion
I worship life
Anatomy went crazy with me
I'm all heart

IMITACIÓN DE LI PO

A Rodolfo Hinostroza

Pomo en mano le canto a la luna
Contemplando azorado su piel de cascada
    / sus montañas hondas /
Su ojo en mis ojos me deslumbra
        ¡Hurra!
Me vengo / chupándole el culo a la luna
Pomo en mano / la noche revela los sudores del día
El veneno :: la música
toda flor del camino
son lunares eternos
¡cuerda para saltar!
abandono al recuerdo
De repente / mi mano blande—glande seguro—
1 onírica espada de nieve
La luna me besa
Mis barbas relumbran
:: Estoy & no estoy ::
Afiebradamente transparente
Descubro a mi doble tañendo 1 laúd
Abriéndose paso en 1 vagina de nubes

IMITATION OF LI PO

To Rodolfo Hinostroza

Bottle in hand I sing to the moon
Nervously contemplating its avalanche skin
     / its deep mountains /
Its eye in my eyes dazzles me
          Hurrah!
I'm coming / sucking the moon's ass
Bottle in hand / the night unmasks the day's sweat
The poison :: music
every roadside flower
is 1 eternal birthmark
1 jump rope!
I abandon the memory
Suddenly / my hand brandishes—cock sure—
1 oneiric sword of snow
The moon kisses me
My beard glistens
:: I'm there & I'm not ::
Feverishly transparent
I discover my double strumming 1 lute
Opening the way inside 1 vagina of clouds

ÚLTIMA ELEGÍA A JESÚS LUIS BENÍTEZ

El día en que tuviste que morirte
no fue el que habías elegido siglos antes
Sobraban las ganas & los astros
1 hueco profundo & 1 ganglio de mujer te estrangularon
¿La botella? / Te ayudó a sobrevivir & a conocernos
Te hubieras enterrado con el feto de tu hijo
    —tu mayor impulso ciego—
O quizás hubieras desnudado para siempre
    las llagas sin remedio de Jimi la Vestida
Jugando—otra vez más—
al pirata que olvida que cantaba
      la balada del *Ceviche Eterno*
Ya tú sabras / en el humo
lo breve del hornazo & sus efluvios
Las palabras / para ti son pedos del negro Charlie Parker
caderas de Dyonisos reencarnado
crucigramas que vibran gota a gota su pezón
/ panales de gaznate mezcaleado /
Entre el Infierno & el Sanedrín
entra volando 1 venado en las cavernas de Altamira
Los volcanes descansan dibujando su próximo sueño
Las leyes de Newton juegan billar con el núcleo de esta bola negra
Tú celebras el misterio con tus greñas
Besando poro a poro la explosión-comunión del laberinto
Llueve / mientras vives
& aún de tus cenizas brota el gesto
con que borran *lo que* sea los diluvios
Que nos explique todo esto Roland Barthes
Que se reten a muerte la mentira & el fundillo
Ya va siendo hora de prender la prójima bacha
& dinamitar la güeva que congela la magia de este tren

LAST ELEGY TO JESÚS LUIS BENÍTEZ*

The day you had to die
wasn't the 1 you'd chosen centuries before
Stars & desires were left over
1 profound void & the ganglion of 1 woman strangled you
The bottle? / It helped you survive & get to know us
You'd have buried yourself with your son's fetus
      —your greatest blind impulse—
Or perhaps you'd have exposed once & for all
    Jimi la Vestida's incurable sores
Playing—once again—
the pirate who forgets he was singing
    the ballad of the *Eternal Ceviche*
By now you must know / in the smoke
how brief are the stench & its effluvia
Words / for you they're Charlie Parker's farts
the thighs of Dionysius reincarnate
crosswords that vibrate his nipples drop by drop
/ mezcalinized throat honeycombs /
Between Hell & the Sanhedrin
1 stag flies into the Altamira caves
Volcanos repose & design their next dream
Newton's laws shoot pool with the 8-ball's nucleus
You consecrate the pascal mystery with your nappy hair
Kissing each pore of the labyrinth's communion-explosion
It rains / while you're alive
& from your very ashes blooms the gesture
by which the floods erase *whatever* it is
Let Roland Barthes explain it all to us
Let the lie & the backside challenge each other to the death
It's high time to spark up old lady roach
& dynamite the bullshit congealing the magic of this train

* Jesús Luis Benítez (1949–1980) was a Mexican writer closely associated with the countercultural literary and artistic movement of the late 1960s and early 1970s, *La Onda* [The Wave].

¡OH VENAS! / HERMANAS DE LAS DE PAUL VERLAINE

Alcohol : áspero : & suntuoso
rotundo alcohol sin órbitas / con flujos /
viajando adentro de tu manantial alado
hoy sólo te bebo
que te adjetive 1 chango
Claro sol / marino / subcutáneo
volcánico / gandalla / & operístico
Meado espejo de mis muecas
Hoy que te escribo te regalo un 4
Me sirvo de tu voz para que hables
Mojado en tus cabellos me descráneo
Vuelo en el gatillo de tu fuego
De 1 gajo a otro de tu tibio boquete hasta el desagüe
Garabato de nervios despeinados
Hermano liendre-alcohol
Carnal machete presentido & heredado
A contraluz / te estoy / cantando

OH VEINS! / SISTERS OF THE VEINS OF PAUL VERLAINE

Alcohol : harsh : & sumptuous
resounding orbitless alcohol / with flows /
traveling inside your winged wellspring
today I drink only you
let them call you 1 ape
Bright sun / aquatic / subcutaneous
volcanic / delinquent / operatic
Piss-soaked mirror of my grimaces
While I'm writing you now I'll let you take the rap
I'll help myself to your voice so you can speak
Drenched in your hair I lose my skull
I fly on the trigger you pull
From 1 slice of your tepid hole to another down the drain
Scribble of disheveled nerves
Louse-alcohol brother
Comrade machete foretold & passed down
Against the light / to you I / sing

CARTA ABIERTA A KENNETH REXROTH

Sin 1 tornado que enarene su garganta
este planeta gime / ayuno de jardines & asideros
La nieve enlodada : los párpados vencidos
Tam-táms de Áfricas internas
no han logrado trocar su peste en rosas
su humareda enemiga de fragancias
en suaves remolinos / donde sólo la bruja chispa del deseo alumbre
     & se desmande
Las cabras & los toros arrancados de su cielo
piden limosna en dispensarios / mataderos / mercados de forraje
bailarinas ves llorando / congeladas /
tragafuegos dibujándose en sus ingles
mares de pie & asfaltos de no entienden
comedores de plátanos con playeras que dicen: *Hegel vitamínico*
& 1000 & 1 atrocidades
con su talco coagulado / como único bolsillo
Si la materia fuera cíclope
éste no sería su ojo
Gorila destronado
Nereida ya marchita
Horca resucitándose
para mejor burlarse de sus propias células colgadas
Calistenia trágica de paracaídas atorados
Bajo 1 lluvia de excrementos
/ mezcla de catsup e intestinos de gorrión /
que no puede detener ni siquiera 1 sortilegio de gitana

OPEN LETTER TO KENNETH REXROTH

Without 1 tornado to sand down its throat
this planet moans / diet of gardens & toeholds
Dirty snow : beaten eyelids
Tom-toms of internal Africas
haven't managed to turn its plague to roses
its haze the enemy of fragrance
in gentle windmills / where only the wicked spark of desire ignites
      & runs wild
Goats & bulls ripped from their heaven
beg for alms in dispensary / slaughterhouse / feed market
you see ballerinas crying / frozen /
fire-eaters drawing pictures in their groins
seas of feet & blacktops that don't understand
banana eaters with tee shirts saying: *Hegel vitamins*
& 1,000 & 1 atrocities
with their coagulated talc / as their only pocket
If matter were 1 cyclops
this wouldn't be its eye
Dethroned gorilla
Withered nereid
Resuscitating noose
the better to mock its own dangling cells
Tragic calisthenics of 1 tangled parachute
Under 1 rain of excrement
/ mixture of catsup & hummingbird guts /
that can't deflect even 1 gypsy woman's curse

¿TE HAS FIJADO CÓMO EL SENA YA NO NOS MIRA A LOS OJOS & LA GARE DE LYON LA HAN LLENADO CON PROPAGANDA OFRECIÉNDO $$ POR LA CAPTURA DE LA BANDA BAADER-MEINHOF?

Para Frank Venaille & Paul Tillman

Acaricio mi próximo suicidio
como mi poema más punzocortante
como mi poema más perfecto
En las butacas-Kenacort & Valium 10
de 1 baratísimo cine de Barbes-Rochechouart
besando con besos de rata rabiosamente blanca
los muslos-maceta de flores
de Margarita / dueña & señora de mis risas
& la acaricio : la acaricio
como 1 borracho su hígado deshecho
o 1 expulsado del Partido Comunista
la voz con que gritó: *A la mierda con Marx*
se lo lavan con orines de Utopía
& si la película de Bogart la pasan fracturada o casi ciega
o la flauta mágica de hash
no alcanza a tapizar con doblones españoles
el crecido—hinchadísimo—galeón de mis pulmones
Qué acción heroica
qué mueca keatoniana
      va a quedarnos
sino la de tendernos catalepticaluciferinamente
            en posición de muertos
sobre el lomo-sal reseca de 1 vía de ferrocarril imaginaria
& ahí / desde esa posición / desde ese encierro
pasearnos nuestra pata menos acalambrada
por el foco menos fundido de los ojos
& que el pelo de la mollera se confunda con el pelo de los güevos
las erupciones del Monte de Venus

DID YOU NOTICE HOW THE SEINE DOESN'T LOOK US IN THE EYE ANYMORE & HOW THEY FILLED THE GARE DE LYON WITH PROPAGANDA OFFERING $$ FOR THE CAPTURE OF THE BAADER-MEINHOF GANG?

For Frank Venaille & Paul Tillman

I embrace my next suicide
as my sharpest poem
my consummate poem
In the Kenacort & Valium-10 seats
of 1 cut-rate cinema at Barbès & Rochechouart
kissing with rabid-white rat kisses
Daisy's flowering thighs /
mistress & queen of my laughter
& I embrace her : I embrace her
as 1 lush embraces his rotten liver
or 1 exile from the Communist Party
embraces the voice that screamed: *To hell with Marx*
he's washed in the piss of Utopia
& if they think the Bogart film's damaged or washed out
or the magic flute of hash
can't quite cover the swollen—bulging—
galleon of my lungs in Spanish doubloons
What heroic act
what keatonesque face
   will be left to us
but the 1 where we catalepticoluciferianistically
         position ourselves like corpses
on the saltback of 1 imaginary railroad
& there / from that position / from that enclosure
walk our least gnarled paw
across the least melted spotlight of our eyes
until we can't tell the hairs on our head from the hair on our balls
the eruptions of Mount Venus

con la lava de la Mente-Rajatabla
Mientras cantamos con el estómago vacío
1 champurrado eufórico de la rola: *There's no future*
           & nos tiramos a fondo
¿pozos? / ¿buzos? / ¿gambusinos? / ¿tlachiqueros de qué?

from the lava of the Vigilant Mind
While we sing on empty stomachs
1 euphoric thick hot cacao of a tune: *There's no future*
            & plunge to the bottom
wells? / divers? / goldminers? / *tlachiqueros** of what?

* A *tlachiquero* extracts the sap of the maguey, called *aguamiel* [honeywater], from
which pulque is made.

A LA MEMORIA DE GERARD DE NERVAL

La imaginación humana no ha inventado nada
que no sea cierto / en este mundo o en los otros

La imaginación se rapa el cráneo
/ en este mundo & en los otros /
Derruido el estanquillo
vuelto 1 denso panal la coraza del changarro
Las pestañas metálicas : enemigas de la sed & de los créditos
como en las afueras de los burdeles de Indonesia
nomás están mirando
La imaginación rapada
se sigue levantando las entradas a sus sótanos
con 1 hoja de afeitar de mantarrayas
Con la hoja de afeitar de sus entrañas
la imaginación te está carneando
A esta hora fritanguera / extremaunciosa
en esta ciudad sin flotación
en esta ciudad de nervios náufragos
con la imaginación no vas a hablar de muslos barnizados en el sándalo
La tal ivaginación isotopútrida
la tal ivaginación que te es tan última estación
tu yoyo alado
ni en el reclu va a cantarte *tú si puedes*
o la haces mi Campeón / si nomás no
si nomás no & subrayado
A esta hora fritanguera / extremaunciosa
en esta ciudad sin flotación
en esta ciudad de nervios náufragos
la tal ivaginación ya sin rezagos
te alcanza por el empeine de los ojos
¿Qué estas tocando?
Aquí ni las maracas ni el paisaje
ni haber cogido bajo minas

TO THE MEMORY OF GÉRARD DE NERVAL

The human imagination hasn't invented anything
untrue / in this world or any other

Imagination shaves its skull
/ in this world & the others /
The gutted newsstand
becomes 1 crowded hive the shell of 1 bodega
Metallic eyelashes : enemies of thirst & credit
as in the red-light districts of Indonesia
they're only looking
The shaven imagination
keeps raising the doorways to its basements
with 1 stingray's razorblade
With its entrails' razorblade
imagination butchers you
At this hour of fried street food / extreme unction
in this city without flotation
this city of shipwrecked nerves
you don't speak with imagination about burnished sandalwood thighs
That isotoputrid invagination
that same invagination you so think is the last stop
even in the slammer your winged yoyo
won't sing to you *if you can*
or if you do my Champion / or if you can't anymore
if you can't anymore is underlined
At this hour of fried street food / extreme unction
in this city without flotation
this city of shipwrecked nerves
that same invagination but no longer lagging behind
grabs you by the arches of your eyes
What are you playing?
No maracas here no landscape
no getting laid under minefields

ni la burra ilusión de los alfanjes
El degollado terco en soñar / sueña su sangre
Gotea & regala si la vagancia le ha dado ejemplos tales
Pero en verdad sólo si ella
lo ha cobijado / arrastrarando
el nido de éter que es su desastre

& no stupid illusion of scimitars
The man with the cut throat dreams stubbornly on / his blood dreams
It trickles & yields if delinquency has given him such models
But in reality only if it
gave him shelter / dragging
the ethereal nest of his disaster

REVOLUCIONES & ESTATUS / IBAN & VENÍAN

Entonces el aire era 1 cangrejo resbalándose de la cresta de mi ola
el magnetismo de los poros / de las calles / de los gritos & los charcos
se había arrugado como el clima llamado de los pies sobre los cuellos
En las camas los pantanos no dejaban tocar a gusto la pianola del
      jadeo
                    La luna supuraba
Venadeaba la guerrilla a los ríos turbios
                  Flotaba niebla & en exceso
Naves espaciales hinchaban—diarrea de hormigueros—nuestros sueños
& hasta en las sordomudeces de los cines interrumpían la humedad de
nuestra navaja erótica las risas ametralladas de los muertos

STATUS & REVOLUTIONS / CAME & WENT

Back then air was 1 crab sliding off the crest of my wave
the magnetic pull of pores / of streets / of puddles & screams
was shriveled like the so-called climate of feet upon necks
Snug in our beds the swamps played 1 wheezing pianola nonstop
                    The moon festered
They hunted the guerrillas into turbid rivers for the kill
                    Fog hovered—excessively
Spaceships swelled our dreams—with anthill diarhhea
& even the moviehouse deaf-mutenesses were invaded by our erotic
switchblade's wetness / the machine-gunned laughter of the dead

PARA NUESTRA SEÑORA DE GUADALUMPEN

Por el manto cumbiambero de mi virgen
por su sexy morenía
por su aparición tan espectral
en el tiempo en el que herraban
los corazones de mi savia
& los cerros se cubrían de gemidos e impiedad

Por el halo de tzentzontles con que hablaba
Cantadito como en barrio lagunero
o en fandango de nopal
Negra perla / faz briosa
Mancha húmeda
he venido estas "Mañanitas" a clamar
Mexicanos de hasta abajo
teoyótls desvanecidos
desde el cráter de la herida
la venimos a invocar

No que perros la transporten
o en la feria de su espíritu se revenda el nanacátl
Nuestra entrega es flor sedosa
Guerra abierta a la boñiga del corral

Por mirar de frente su solar descompostura
larva ella que trastorna
la severa senilidad de los magueyes
agua regia que bebemos
como a vulva de panal

Niña ella de los cielos
travesura-sed embriagapuertas

TO OUR LADY OF GUADALUMPEN

For my virgin's cumbia shawl
for her brown-skinned sexiness
for her spectral apparition
when they were nailing horseshoes
in the my lifeblood's hearts
& the hills rang with groans & blasphemies

For the halo of mockingbirds she spoke with
In the singsong of backwater towns
or the nopal fandango
Black pearl / flushed face
Damp stain
I've come to declaim these daybreak serenades
Mexicans from rock bottom
vanished divinities
from the crater of the wound
we come to summon her

So the dogs don't carry her off
so they don't peddle shrooms at her spirit's festival
We present her with flowers of silk
Open war on the cow shit of corrals

Looking straight at her solar decomposure
she's the larva that plagues
the grave senility of magueys
the royal water we drink
as from 1 beehive's vulva

This daughter of the heavens
this deviance-thirst that intoxicates gates

A los pies de su misterio
nos venimos a inclinar

Quiera la raíz de nuestro ojo no negarla ni evadirla
Arde su ala / la llamarada de su brisa
Su petate es mi petate
Nuestra boda / celestial

At the feet of her mystery
we come to bow down

May the root of our eye neither scorn nor avoid her
Blazing her wing / the flame of the breeze
Her bedroll is my bedroll
Our marriage / celestial

ADOLESCENCIA BISIESTA

Para Blaise Cendrars

Trabajaba entonces con cincel de kryptonita verde
    / fino & dañino /
Como pocos dientes de coyote
Como pocas ¡pocas! bolsas marsupiales
Acariciaba mi bragueta adelante & detrás de las ventanas
Novias chinas: golpe de suerte
& estribillos de esa índole
Escalinatas de Metro: mis sonrisas
Toboganes de espuma: mis miradas
Compases de 1000 puntas / cada paso
Martillos sin 1 clavo pero lluvias muy muy lluvias mis bolsillos
Poesía crecía en belleza
Dormir era 1 despertar / en sus alvéolos
Manotearse el pelo: rehiletear 1 ojo
escupir caminos para los que chingan más que salvan los zapatos
¡Dinero gratis! ¡autopistas gratis!
¡Aventones para Monte Albán!
Me enamoraba de llamas
Conversaba con ciempiés
Grababa en piel de yunque el chismorreo monosílabo que trompetean
    los semáforos
La ciudad me era tan labio / tan capullo / tan pezón
Jugaba con la doña a *la pared & los orines*
Hemoglobina no bajaba de ocurrente
Respirar me era tan Mark Twain / tan William Burroughs
    ...Burra cargada de...
Botella con mecha interna & hacia afuera
El desierto ¡por fin! derrotado por la voz
Mi pata de mambo: puro calcio
poniéndole semillas a la tierra
cascabeles a los botes

LEAP YEAR ADOLESCENCE

For Blaise Cendrars

Back then I worked with 1 kryptonite chisel
     / more sharp-edged & deadly /
Than most coyote teeth
Than any marsupial's pouch
I stroked the fly of my pants in front of windows & behind them
Chinese brides: lucky strike
& refrains of that sort
Subway stairs: my smiles
Foaming slides: my glances
1,000-pointed compasses / every step
Hammers with no nails but with rains heavy rains in my pockets
Poetry grew in beauty
To sleep was to wake up / in its alveoli
To shake my hair: to dart 1 eye
to spit out streets for those who'd rather fuck around than save their shoes
Free money! free highways!
Free lifts to Monte Albán!
I fell in love with llamas
Conversed with centipedes
Engraved in jungle flesh the monosyllabic gossip streetlights trumpet
The city was all lip / all prick / all tit to me
I played *the wall & the piss* with the Mrs.
Hemoglobin was 1 joke that never got old
For me breathing was so Mark Twain / so William Burroughs
     …She-ass carrying…
Bottle bomb & moving outward
The desert—finally!—crushed by the voice
My mambo paw: pure calcium
putting seeds in the earth
sleigh bells on boats

—disecando las baterías del adefesio—
Electrificando el espacio de los bailes
única & solamente con giros populares
Muy muy muy acompañado recalentado invadido de mí

—dissecting monstrosity's batteries—
Electrifying the dance hall
with nothing more than popular turns of phrase
Very very heavily seasoned reheated & laced with myself

CARTE D'IDENTITÉ

Si puedes ser leyenda
Para qué ser fosa común

Mario Santiago Papasquiaro / infrarrealista de 1ª hora ((milita en este movimiento trepidatorio desde su fundación en 1975)) emitió su Aullido de Cisne primigenio en la Ciudad de México—capital de los humillados a raíz—en medio de 1 tormenta eléctrica / la madrugada del 24 de diciembre de 1953—año de la muerte de Dylan Thomas & Jorge Negrete—.

La cuerda del eco de ese *tour de fórceps a capella* ((bizonte burilado en la placenta de Altamira)) retumba en el violín de Ingres de estas páginas / que a ojo de buen cubero concentran apenas el 10% de los glóbulos rojos de su ópera primate.

Serpiente de agua en el horóscopo chino / *Ocelote* en el náhuatl / *Capricornio* en el occidental / fue en su infancia seguidor de las glorias del *Rebaño Sagrado* del Guadalajara & en su 1ª juventud subía y bajaba ((*sin timón & en el delirio*)) por las serpientes & escaleras escherianas de la *Dialéctica de la Naturaleza*—este desmadre desigual & combinado—con tal impulso / que sólo la revelación que le transmitiera el chaneque brigadier José Revueltas: *La tragedia de la especie humana es su carencia de sí* lo mantuvo con los pies alados sosteniendo el peso drenado de su cerebelo abierto.

Hoy / mañana & siempre.
Antipoeta & vago insobornable / prófugo de la Nada / ajolote en 1 cascada de aire.

Lo que más ama en la marejada de la vida:
Las hembras platívolas que no cesan de minar la masmédula mítica de los habitantes de esta galaxia-Oliverio Girondo.
Su profesión es darse cuenta.

CARTE D'IDENTITÉ

If you can be 1 legend
Why be 1 mass grave

Mario Santiago Papasquiaro / frontline infrarealist ((who has fought in this turbulent movement since its inception in 1975)) released his primordial Swan's Howl in Mexico City—capitol of the nakedly debased—in the midst of 1 electrical storm / at dawn on the morning of December 24, 1953—the year of the death of Dylan Thomas & Jorge Negrete—.

The echoing string of this *a cappella tour de forceps* ((1 buffalo carved in the placenta of Altamira)) reverberates in the Ingres violin of these pages / which by 1 rough estimation contain scarcely 10% of his primate opera's red blood cells.

Water serpent in the Chinese horoscope / *Ocelot* in the Náhuatl / *Capricorn* in the occidental / in his childhood he followed Guadalajara's triumphant *Rebaño Sagrado** & in his early youth he rose & fell ((*delirious & rudderless*)) through the Escherian snakes & ladders of the Dialectics of Nature—that composite & uneven pandemonium—with such force / that only the revelation transmitted by the *chaneque*** brigadier José Revueltas: *The tragedy of the human species is its lack of itself* kept his winged feet supporting the drained weight of his open cerebellum.

Today / tomorrow & always.
Antipoet & incorruptible bum / fugitive from the Void / salamander in 1 waterfall of air.

What he most loves in the whirlpool of life:
The flying saucer women ceaselessly mining the mythic moremarrow of this Oliverio Girondo galaxy's inhabitants.
His profession is noticing.

Su verdad / ninguna.

Su número teosófico: el 69.

Su *alter ego* / sueño & guía:

Edmundo Dantés / Conde de Montecristo.

Su máxima ilusión: meterle 1 gol de corner a la ausencia flagrante del viento de Diós Campeador.

Escribe como camina / a ritmo de chile frito.

A tranco firme & sin doblarse.

Entre 1976 & 1978 vivió como chupamirto / olisqueando los puntos cardinales de su laboratorio-aprendizaje: París / Viena / Barcelona & Jerusalem.

Su mujer le dice de cariño: *Ojos de nutria / Boca de glande.*

His truth / there isn't 1.

His theosophical number: 69.

His *alter ego* / dream & guide:

Edmond Dantès / The Count of Monte Cristo.

His grand illusion: to score 1 corner kick goal in the flagrant absence of the Field God's wind.

He writes like he walks / to the beat of 1 roving brass band.
              With firm & unbending stride.

Between 1976 & 1978 he lived like 1 hummingbird / scenting the cardinal points of his apprentice's lab: Paris / Vienna /
              Barcelona & Jerusalem.

His wife affectionately calls him: *Otter eyes / Cock mouth.*

---

* *El Rebaño Sagrado* [The Holy Flock] is the nickname of the Guadalajara soccer team, *Las Chivas* [The Goats].

**Chaneque are elf-like, mythical creatures associated with elemental forces in Mexican folklore.

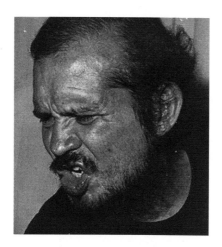

THE AUTHOR

Mario Santiago Papasquiaro was born in Mexico City in 1953 and attended Juan Bañuelos's poetry workshop at UNAM. In 1975, he and a group of friends—Mara Larrosa, José Peguero, and Rubén Medina along with Chileans Roberto Bolaño, Bruno Montané Krebs, and Juan Esteban Harrington—founded the radical poetry movement, Infrarealism. Santiago Papasquiaro's poems were first published in the journals *Pájaro de calor* (1976) and *Correspondencia infra* (1977) and the anthology *Muchachos desnudos bajo el arco iris de fuego* (1979). The chapbook *Beso eterno* and the book-length collection *Aullido de cisne* were published by Al Este del Paráiso in 1995 and 1996, respectively. In 1998, Santiago Papasquiaro was killed by a car while walking in Mexico City. In 2008, the Fondo de Cultura Económica published his posthumous anthology *Jeta de santo*, edited by Mario Raúl Guzmán and the poet's widow, Rebeca López. In 2008, the collection *Respiración del laberinto* appeared in its first Cartonera edition. In 2012, Ediciones sin fin published Santiago Papasquiaro's long poem *Sueño sin fin*, edited by Bruno Montané Krebs. That same year, Almadía released the collection *Arte & Basura,* edited by Luis Felipe Fabre. In 2016, Matadero published Santiago Papasquiqro's groundbreaking long poem *Consejos de 1 discípulo de Marx a 1 fanático de Heidegger,* edited by Rubén Medina.

THE TRANSLATOR

Cole Heinowitz is a poet, translator, scholar, and professor of literature at Bard College. She is the author of two books of poetry, *The Rubicon* (The Rest, 2008) and *Daily Chimera* (Incommunicado, 1995), and the chapbook *Stunning in Muscle Hospital* (Detour, 2002). Heinowitz is the translator of Mario Santiago Papasquiaro's *Advice from 1 Disciple of Marx to 1 Heidegger Fanatic* (Wave Books, 2013) and *Beauty Is Our Spiritual Guernica* (Commune Editions, 2015), as well as *A Tradition of Rupture: Selected Critical Writings of Alejandra Pizarnik* (Ugly Duckling Presse, 2019). Her book-length study, *Spanish America and British Romanticism, 1777-1826: Rewriting Conquest,* was published by Edinburgh University Press in 2010. Heinowitz's recent poems, translations, and essays can be found in *Letters for Olson* (Spuyten Duyvil, 2016), *The Chicago Review* (2017), *Erizo: A Journal of the Arts* (2018), *Two Lines* (2018), *19th-Century Contexts* (2018), *Harper's Magazine, The Wordsworth Circle* (2019), and *A Cultural History of Tragedy in the Age of Empire* (Bloomsbury, 2019).

The Cliff Becker Book Prize in Translation

"Translation is the medium through which American readers gain greater access to the world. By providing us with as direct a connection as possible to the individual voice of the author, translation provides a window into the heart of a culture."
—Cliff Becker, May 16, 2005

Cliff Becker (1964–2005) was the National Endowment for the Arts Literature Director from 1999 to 2005. He began his career at the NEA in 1992 as a literature specialist, was named Acting Director in 1997, and in 1999 became the NEA's Director of Literature.

The publication of this book of translation is a reflection of Cliff's passionate belief that the arts must be accessible to a wide audience and not subject to vagaries of the marketplace. During his tenure at the NEA, he expanded support for individual translators and led the development of the NEA Literature Translation Initiative. His efforts did not stop at the workplace, however. He carried his passion into the kitchen as well as into the board room. Cliff could often be seen at home relaxing in his favorite, worn-out, blue T-shirt, which read, "Art Saves Me!" He truly lived by this credo. To ensure that others got the chance to have their lives impacted by uncensored art, Cliff hoped to create a foundation to support the literary arts which would not be subject to political changes or fluctuations in patronage, but would be marked solely for the purpose of supporting artists, and in particular, the creation and distribution of art which might not otherwise be available. While he could not achieve this goal in his short life, seven years after his untimely passing, his vision was realized.

The Cliff Becker Endowment for the Literary Arts was established by his widow and daughter in 2012 to give an annual publication prize in translation in his memory. The Cliff Becker Book Prize in Translation annually produces one volume of literary translation in English. It is our hope that with on-going donations to help grow the Becker Endowment for the Literary Arts, important artists will continue to touch, and perhaps save, lives of those whom they reach through the window of translation.

Donations to The Cliff Becker Endowment for the Literary Arts will help ensure that Cliff's vision continues to enrich our literary heritage. It is more important than ever before that English-speaking readers are able to comprehend our world and our histories through the literatures of diverse cultures. Tax deductible donations to the Endowment will be gratefully received by White Pine Press. Checks should be made payable to White Pine Press and sent to The Cliff Becker Endowment for the Literary Arts, c/o White Pine Press, P.O. Box 236, Buffalo, NY 14201.